'HOW TO'

BOOK OF
RIDING
AND HORSE CARE
HEIDI BEST

BROCKHAMPTON PRESS

'HOW TO'

The 'HOW TO' Book of Riding and Horse Care has been written, designed and illustrated to make the early stages of riding and the basic aspects of stable work, clear, straightforward and explicit. Used as an accompaniment to riding instruction, it will make the process of learning more enjoyable and satisfying.

Contents

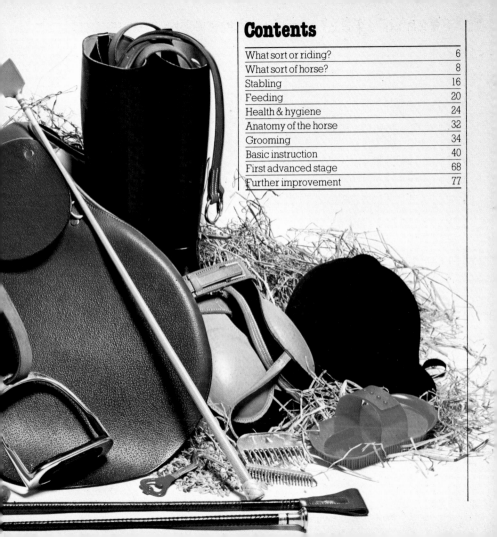

The 'How To' Book of Riding and Horse Care
was conceived, edited and designed by
Simon Jennings and Company Limited

This edition published 1996 by
Brockhampton Press Ltd,
20 Bloomsbury Street,
London WC1B 3QA

Text and illustrations
© 1981 Simon Jennings & Co Ltd

ISBN 1 86019 254 8

Printed and bound in U.A.E.

THE AUTHOR
Despite a non-horsy
background, Heidi Best
has always loved horses
and started riding at the
age of eight. She now
enjoys competing on her
threequarter-bred mare,
Moondancer.
Until recently, she was the
Assistant Editor of *Pony*
and *Light Horse*
magazines. She now works
freelance from home, and
is a member of the British
Equestrian Writers'
Association.
She also instructs regularly
at Saltford Riding Club
near Bath and teaches the
Mendip Farmers' Hunt
pony club.

Introduction

No book can ever replace the help given by an experienced instructor, but it can provide a valuable aid to the young and the novice rider – especially as a visual check on correct and incorrect techniques. This book has been written and designed to help all inexperienced riders to assess their progress and make the most of the instruction they are receiving.

Riding is one of the most rapidly growing leisure interests – a factor which has led to a considerable increase in the number of public riding establishments and schools. There is some evidence to suggest that instructors cannot be trained fast enough to cope with the demand. Nevertheless, for children who do not have experienced riders in the family – and adults who have decided to take up riding, there are few satisfactory alternatives to approved riding schools. The importance of correct and thorough instruction is stressed everywhere today – just as it is in this book – and there are no short cuts to competence in riding.

This book will, however, answer many of the questions that novices will raise during a course of instruction, and help them to be prepared for the next stage. Most riders, once they have established a 'feel' for the horse, and mastered some of the basic techniques, progress rapidly. Once they know what a correct action feels like, they seldom get it wrong again, and they can look forward to continuing steady improvement. And it is the satisfaction of improving – in control of the horse and by extending the range of one's capabilities in the saddle – that makes riding a life-long pleasure.

This book will help you decide whether you should become a horse owner, what sort of riding you want to do and how much time you will have to devote to it all. It will introduce you to the problems and pleasures of stable management, and all the related aspects of feeding, health, grooming and care of tack. Riding is an expensive pastime, but there are several levels at which you can approach it. This book will help you to find that level.

What sort of riding?

There is a variety of reasons why all sorts of people, from all walks of life, decide that they would like to learn to ride. Some simply like the idea of a pleasant hack once a week in the countryside, requiring only a quiet, reliable mount to transport them gently for an hour or so before lunch. Others may have aspirations to own a horse or pony, possibly to hunt or take part in competitive events, and must be prepared to spend far more time and money in order to gain the required proficiency. In all cases, the basic techniques, which must be learned before you can progress to your chosen activity, are the same.

There is another group of people to whom an introduction to riding is an entrance to another world: the disabled. A reliable, generous horse or pony gives mentally and physically handicapped adults and children therapy and pleasure combined. The physically handicapped become mobile, on a par with riders without handicaps; those with learning difficulties find an absorbing and pleasurable interest; the blind enjoy riding and are able to 'see' their mount by feel.

Whatever the reasons for wanting to learn to ride, a vast reservoir of pleasure and discovery opens before you.

Riding ambitions
Most riders will never aspire to anything more adventurous than a quiet hack in the countryside, *above,* but for those who are more ambitious there are many possibilities. Show jumping, *right,* attracts more young riders than ever before and may be approached through riding club and Pony Club activities. Polo, *top left,* remains the sport of the rich, but some forms of racing, *bottom left,* are open to amateurs – especially point-to-point and hunt racing. Even as a spectator, however, the beginner or weekend rider will learn from equestrian sports. But there are many local shows, gymkhanas and hunter trials which give novices a chance to compete. They also provide opportunities for children.

What sort of horse?

Buying and keeping a horse is a very costly business, and it is vital that you buy something suited to your standard of riding and knowledge. Probably the best way of buying a horse is by word of mouth. You may hear of someone who is parting with their horse and they will probably be just as anxious as you to establish that it is suitable. Another way of buying a horse is through advertisements in the horsy press or local newpapers. A reputable horse dealer may have something suitable for you in his yard, but do make sure that his reputation is justified.

Buying a riding-school horse can be successful, but beware, because a horse that behaves under supervision may be an absolute pig in a different environment. Horse sales are for experts only and should be avoided. In any case, whichever source you use, it is advisable to take someone knowledgeable with you.

A young horse is unsuitable for a novice rider because it will undoubtedly be 'green', and require handling and schooling which your inexperience will render you unable to give. The most suitable age for a first horse is over eight years because it will know its job and hopefully be schooled well enough for you to ride and handle it with ease. An elderly horse should be avoided. It will require extra

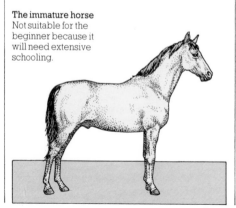

The immature horse
Not suitable for the beginner because it will need extensive schooling.

The mature horse
Horses aged eight years or more, if they have no bad habits, should be suitable for novices.

care to keep it in good health, and will obviously be limited in the amount of work it can do.

A horse that is too big will be uncomfortable to ride, and control will be impaired if your legs don't reach down to the girth region. Apart from being unable to carry your weight without strain, a horse that is too small will be equally uncomfortable, and will probably make you feel quite unsafe.

Before handing over money for your chosen horse, ask your veterinary surgeon to look at it. An unsound horse is useless, so *never* buy a horse without having it vetted first.

The old horse
A horse that is too old for the job will probably appear rather bony and lacking in substance.

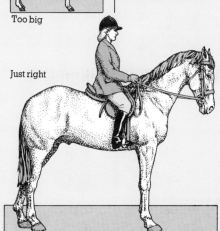

CHOOSING THE RIGHT SIZE

Too small

Too big

Just right

Made to measure
Since horses and ponies come in all sizes, there is no need to be stuck with one that is too big or too small. The rider's heel should reach the lower part of the girth without stretching, and without having to drastically shorten the leathers. This does not mean that the rider should not ride horses of differing sizes. The important thing is to be able to maintain a comfortable control.

Horses for riding

A horse stands over 14.2 h.h. (there are four inches in a hand), and a pony 14.2 h.h. or under, although some pony breeds do occasionally exceed the 14.2 h.h. limit.

There are several different types of riding horse, and many of them have some, or all, thoroughbred blood. The thoroughbred traces its ancestry back to three foundation Arabs, the Godolphin Arabian, the Byerley Turk and the Darley Arabian, introduced to England at the end of the 17th and beginning of the 18th century.

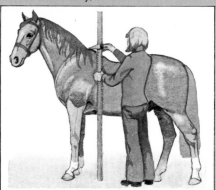

Measuring horses: The height of a horse is measured in hands, the measurement taken from the highest point of the withers to the ground.

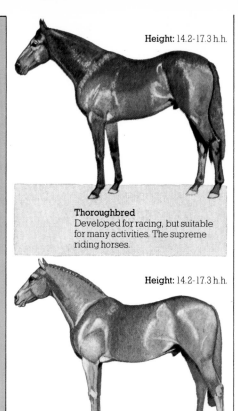

Height: 14.2-17.3 h.h.

Thoroughbred
Developed for racing, but suitable for many activities. The supreme riding horses.

Height: 14.2-17.3 h.h.

Hunter
Often thoroughbreds, but may be halfbred. Strength and endurance are the main requirements.

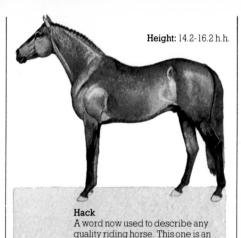

Height: 14.2-16.2 h.h.

Hack
A word now used to describe any quality riding horse. This one is an Anglo-Arab.

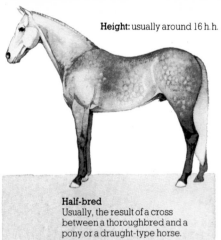

Height: usually around 16 h.h.

Half-bred
Usually, the result of a cross between a thoroughbred and a pony or a draught-type horse.

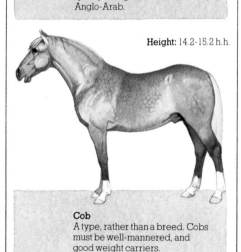

Height: 14.2-15.2 h.h.

Cob
A type, rather than a breed. Cobs must be well-mannered, and good weight carriers.

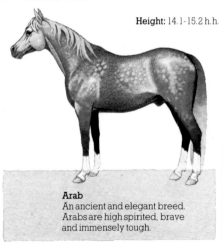

Height: 14.1-15.2 h.h.

Arab
An ancient and elegant breed. Arabs are high spirited, brave and immensely tough.

Owning a horse

Buying and keeping a horse of your own is costly in both time and money but the rewards are enormous, especially if you look after it entirely on your own. If you can't do this, the alternative is to keep your horse at approved livery stables. Unfortunately, this is very expensive, but for those who work long hours, it offers the security of knowing that your horse is in good hands.

If you are looking after your horse, it is important to work out a daily routine suitable to both of you, and to stick to it. The horse has a very accurate 'body-clock', and if you upset his routine by giving him meals at odd times, or varying your arrival time in the morning, he will find this upsetting, and won't thrive. Ideally, you should be available to feed your horse three or four times per day, although you can get away with two visits if the horse is turned-out in a field during the day.

The decision as to whether your horse will be kept in a stable or kept at grass will probably be determined by the amount of time you have to look after it. Unless you are able to devote at least half a normal working day to stable routines and exercise, you should not consider a stable-kept horse.

OWNING A HORSE CHECKLIST OF FINANCIAL COMMITMENTS

PURCHASE PRICE

STABLING

FEEDING

VETERINARY FEES

TACK

TRANSPORTATION

SHOEING

OWNING A HORSE
FINANCIAL AND
PRACTICAL CONSIDERATIONS

Horses and ponies are not cheap. Even a humble children's pony, if it is sound, well-made and not too old, can be expensive.	Do not pay more than you have to: establish the 'market rate' for the type of horse you want and be cautious if the price is higher.
Stabling may not be necessary if you have good pasture available, but a field shelter will be welcome in wintry weather.	If you have stabling – stalls or loose boxes – consider first whether you have the time to give to a stable-kept horse.
Feeding is a regular and increasing expense. The horse's natural diet is grass, but if it is kept in a stable you must provide good	quality hay as well as one or more of the concentrates. These may vary but any horse of 15hh will eat more than 9kg of food each day.
Veterinary fees are unavoidable, though it is to be hoped they do not occur too often. Regular visits for worming and vaccinations must be	allowed for and you should never be reluctant to call the vet because of the probable expense. Delay can be disastrous.
Tack, when it is considered altogether, can cost as much as a pony. Saddle, bridle, headcollar, rugs, tack cleaning and grooming	equipment – and your own riding kit – are all things which you must possess from the outset. There are few short cuts to be made.
Transportation may not be a problem unless you are going to show your horse, hunt, or compete in some other way. If so, you will	need a trailer horsebox and a vehicle powerful enough to pull it. Hiring is possibe almost everywhere, but it is not cheap.
A horse or pony's shoes must be removed at least once every month. The amount you will have to pay will depend upon the average	price charged by farriers in your district – and whether the locality is well-served by farriers. Choose according to recommendation.

Economics

Unless you own a breeding stallion there are no licence fees payable on horses. Every horse owner should take on the responsibility of insuring their horse, not only against theft, injury or death, vet's fees, theft of tack, etc. but also against injury or damage to third persons and their property. Horse insurance is relatively inexpensive (about 6–8% of the animal's value), and the amount of damage a horse can do should it become loose or involved in a road accident, is immense. The chart opposite provides a check list of all the factors which must be taken into account when deciding to become an owner.

Pony breeds

The chief distinction between horses and ponies is one of size. Officially, an animal which is no more than 14.2 h.h. (at the withers) is a pony, anything taller is a horse. This rather obscures the fact that there are many specific pony breeds – some of which, incidentally, occasionally produce animals taller than 14.2 h.h. Among the breeds which produce the best riding ponies are the Shetland, Highland, Fell, Dales, Dartmoor, Exmoor, New Forest, Connemara and Welsh Mountain. These breeds all share the attributes of intelligence, surefootedness and great hardiness, but each is distinctly different in appearance. There are, in fact, four types of Welsh pony: the already mentioned Welsh Mountain (Section A in the Welsh Pony and Cob Society Stud Book), the Welsh Pony (Sec. B), the Welsh Pony of Cob-Type (Sec. C) and the Welsh Cob (Sec. D).

It is mostly by using the Welsh Sec. B or the Dartmoor, that many of the best show ponies are bred. These ponies are shown in three classes:– up to 12.2 h.h., up to 13.2 h.h. and up to 14.2 h.h. They are judged on their manners, conformation and paces.

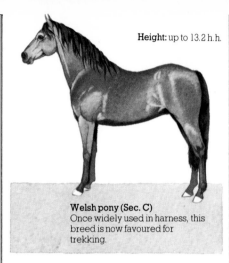

Height: up to 13.2 h.h.

Welsh pony (Sec. C)
Once widely used in harness, this breed is now favoured for trekking.

Height: up to 12.2 h.h.

Dartmoor
Strong and gentle, the Dartmoor is the ideal children's pony. Closely related to the Exmoor.

Height: up to 12 h.h.

Welsh mountain pony (Sec. A)
The most elegant of small ponies.
A very intelligent and durable
type.

Height: 13-14 h.h.

Connemara
An ancient breed, now frequently
crossed with Arabs or
Thoroughbreds. Good jumpers.

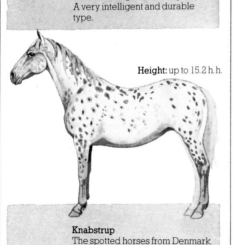

Height: up to 15.2 h.h.

Knabstrup
The spotted horses from Denmark
are pony-sized, though not a true
pony breed.

Height: 14-14.2 h.h.

Dales
These ponies, which are usually
black, are superb working and
riding animals.

Typical stall arrangements

Ring tying method

Log and rope method

Horses in stalls
Stalls consist of individual compartments in a barn-like building. They do not have individual doors, and so the horse must be secured at all times. This is best done by the log and rope method. The 'log' is really a weighty ball which will take up the slack in a rope which is long enough to give the horse maximum freedom within the allotted space. The ring tying method is suitable for securing the horse while cleaning the stall.

Stable construction

There are two main types of stable, the *loose-box*, in which the horse is at liberty to move, roll and lie down at will, or the *stall*, in which he is secured by a log and rope and has to stand or lie in the same place at all times.

A loose-box is obviously the better proposition and should be at least 4 m × 3.5 m (14 ft × 12 ft) for a horse, and 3.5 m × 3 m (12 ft × 10 ft) for a pony.

Doors should be in two parts, at least 1.2 m (4 ft) wide, and open outwards. A narrow door is very dangerous and a horse can hurt and frighten itself considerably if it catches its hip on the way through. Bottom doors should fasten on the outside at the top and bottom with a non-projecting bolt at the top and a foot-operated kick-latch at the bottom, and top doors should be hooked back.

Ventilation is very important and the top door should be left open *all* the time, summer and winter, except perhaps in particularly severe weather if the stable faces north. There should also be an inward-opening window which should be protected on the inside by iron bars. Fresh air is vital, so warmth should be secured by means of extra clothing, not by closing the windows or doors.

THE LOOSE BOX

The loose box is the preferred type of stable, chiefly because the horse does not have to be tethered.

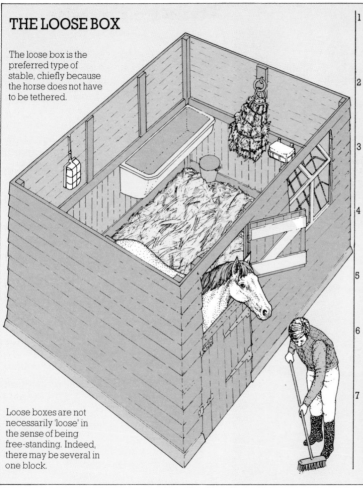

Loose boxes are not necessarily 'loose' in the sense of being free-standing. Indeed, there may be several in one block.

1 **Construction**
Loose boxes may be built of wood, brick or concrete. Single unit types are usually wooden.

2 **Dimensions**
The box should be at least 4m x 3.5m (14ft x 12ft) for a horse, or 3.5m x 3m (12ft x 10ft) for a pony.

3 **Floor**
The stable floor should be of a resilient non-porous material, such as concrete.

4 **Doors & windows**
The door should always be in two parts – the top half remaining open in all but severe weather.

5 **Ventilation**
Living indoors is not natural to horses, so fresh air at all times is vital.

6 **Lighting**
A wall light makes stable work on winter mornings and evenings much easier.

7 **Feeding**
Most stables will have a feeder fixed to the wall and a net for hay. A salt lick, at a convenient height, is a good idea.

The hack

The term hack has several definitions, being the word used to describe any ride taken for pleasure, or any well-mannered horse which gives an enjoyable ride.

It is also the name given to the supreme riding horse of the show-ring, the show hack, which must not exceed 15.3 h.h. and, because it is usually thoroughbred, is generally bay, black, brown, grey or chestnut.

A judge of show hacks will be looking for a blemish-free horse with as near perfect conformation as possible, elegance, beauty, exemplary manners, true level action and an air of grace.

The show hack is not required to jump in the ring, but is ridden in the company of all exhibits in the class at all paces, on both reins, before giving an individual show.

Each horse is then stripped of its saddle, examined by the judge, walked and trotted in-hand, re-saddled and ridden by the judge, then sent out into the ring again to walk and trot around with all the other exhibits, before the final selection is made.

A class of show hacks is a truly elegant sight, the personification of all that is desirable in a riding horse.

Hacks for all

'Hack' is the word applied to any ride which is taken purely for pleasure or recreation and, more specifically, to the quality riding horse of the show ring, *left and below*. The chief requirements are that they should be elegant, well-mannered and smooth actioned. These are the qualities that make 'hacking', *opposite*, a complete pleasure.

Feeding horses & ponies

The foods used for equine feeding are divided into *concentrates* or *bulk*. Concentrates, which include oats, barley, cubes, flaked maize and linseed, are high, by degree, in protein and are fed to horses in hard or fast work, and to mares and growing youngstock.

Bulk foods, which include grass, hay, bran and sugar beet, are vital to the well-being of all horses and ponies because they fill the intestine, keep the digestive process of the body in good working order, and satisfy the horse.

Although there are a number of basic rules which apply to feeding and watering, it must be remembered that each horse and pony is an individual and, as such, will differ in its requirements according to its build, height, temperament, work-load, age, stage of training, and so forth.

BASIC RULES FOR FEEDING

1 Feed little and often, because the horse has a small stomach and is by nature a browsing animal.

2 Feed plenty of bulk to fill the large capacity intestine and aid successful digestion.

3 Feed according to work-load, age, size and temperament.

4 Feed only best quality foodstuffs. Musty or dusty food is low in food content, will impair health if eaten, and may be completely rejected.

5 The horse's stomach lies next to its lungs so always allow at least an hour after feeding before working, otherwise breathing is impaired.

6 Clean, fresh water should be available at *all* times. If this is not possible, then water before feeding.

7 Make no sudden changes in feeding routine.

8 Keep mangers and feeding bowls scrupulously clean by washing after each meal.

9 Try to feed some form of succulent daily, e.g., long grass, sliced carrots, apples, etc.

10 Salt should be added at the rate of approximately one teaspoonful per day to the feed.

FOODSTUFFS

● **Concentrates**
These feeds, which are usually described as 'short' feeds, are the vital sources of energy and nutrition. **Oats** are the best of the concentrates, being very high in protein. They should only be given to horses in work – and sparingly. Too much protein can make horses troublesome. **Barley** and **peas** are both high in protein, but peas give more energy. **Flaked maize** is a good source of energy, but low in protein. **Linseed**, usually fed as jelly or cake, is a good conditioner. **Pony nuts** are a good compound of all the vital nutrients.

● **Bulk foods**
Hay, Which is the main source of bulk, also contains the other elements necessary to keep a horse healthy. It is not sufficient, however, for horses in strong or fast work. **Bran** is a useful bulk food, if not especially nutritious, while **sugar beet** is high in energy. **Chaff** is bulk and very little else.

Pony nuts

Bran

Hay

Linseed

Oats

Sugar beet (dried)

Flaked maize

Peas

Barley

Chaff

Feeding the horse: Horses are grazing animals; they have small stomachs and their natural eating pattern shows a continuous intake of small amounts of food – usually grass. Concentrates, fed in quantities not exceeding 1.8kg (4lbs), can replace a considerable amount of grazing – but a stabled horse will need to be fed up to four times a day and will still consume up to 9kg (20lbs) of hay.

The hunter

Hunting is a traditional countryside sport, and any horse that can follow hounds all day across various types of going, jumping natural obstacles and fences as it goes, is known as a hunter.

The show hunter should convince the judge that it is the sort of horse on which he would like to follow hounds, but is not required to jump in the show-ring.

There are five classes for show hunters: lightweight (in which the horse should be able to carry up to 80 kg (175 lbs), middleweight 80 to 90 kg (175 to 196 lbs), heavyweight 90 kg (196 lbs and over), small (standing between 14.2 h.h. and 15.2 h.h.) and ladies (generally ridden side-saddle).

Show hunters are mainly thoroughbreds, or near thoroughbreds, and should have near-perfect conformation,

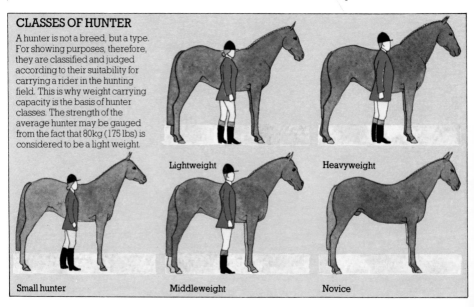

CLASSES OF HUNTER

A hunter is not a breed, but a type. For showing purposes, therefore, they are classified and judged according to their suitability for carrying a rider in the hunting field. This is why weight carrying capacity is the basis of hunter classes. The strength of the average hunter may be gauged from the fact that 80kg (175 lbs) is considered to be a light weight.

Lightweight

Heavyweight

Small hunter

Middleweight

Novice

good manners, and free, on-going paces. Not only must they go forward willingly and freely, but they must also come back and decrease pace easily and obediently.

Watching a class of hunters galloping eagerly round a large, grass arena is an exhilarating experience, and one of the finest of the many grand sights the show-ring can offer.

The Irish hunter
Although not a breed in its own right, the Irish hunter is recognised all over the world as a superb jumper and is much in demand for show jumping. They usually stand 16-17 h.h.

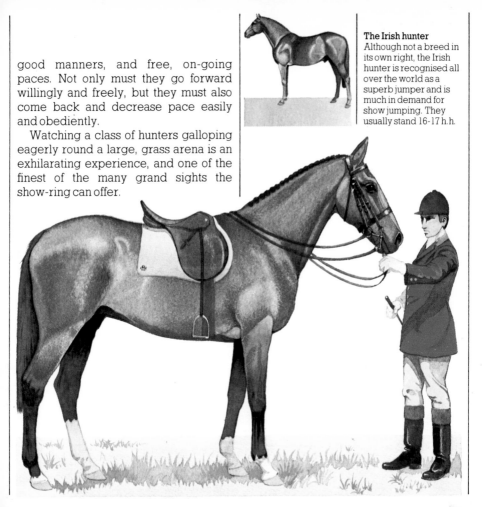

Health & hygiene

All horses suffer from worm infestation, but it is vital that this is kept at an acceptable level by the regular use of *anthelmintics*. The symptoms of an excessive worm burden vary from diarrhoea to blockage, loss of condition and weight, wind problems, anaemia, lethargy, and possible death.

Redworms are the best known and most dangerous of the internal parasites, the others being the large whiteworm, whip or pin worms, lungworm, and tapeworm.

The larvae are picked up when the horse grazes infected pasture and they mature inside the horse, either migrating through, and therefore damaging, the internal organs, or living in the stomach and feeding off its contents. The eggs laid by the mature worm are then passed out with the droppings, causing further pasture infestation.

The larvae obviously cause considerable damage, so prevention is better than cure. All equines, whether kept in or out, should be dosed every six to eight weeks. A variety of worming agents, or anthelmintics, are available, either through your veterinary surgeon or saddlers.

Pasture should be kept clean by the daily removal of all droppings, regular resting, and the grazing of sheep or cattle which will ingest and destroy the larvae which survive only in an equine host.

Vaccinations

Every horse owner should also give consideration to vaccination against equine influenza and tetanus. Equine influenza is highly infectious and even a mild case puts a horse out of action for some considerable time. Tetanus is a killer, and although it can be cured the process is painful and unpleasant.

These vaccines can be given as a combined dose and the initial course of two injections, given four to six weeks apart, is followed by a yearly booster of both vaccines and subsequent annual boosters for influenza, and every three years for tetanus.

You should also have your horse's teeth checked and the sharp edges rasped every six months.

Some veterinary surgeons run schemes whereby they visit every six months to take a worm count, administer vaccinations, and rasp the teeth, and these schemes are obviously well worth subscribing to.

RECOGNISING AILMENTS

A healthy animal has a bright eye, pricked and mobile ears, a glossy coat and carries its head and tail proudly.

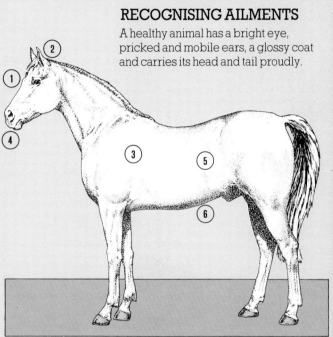

Monitor the health of your horse or pony by checking, regularly, the following points:

1 **Eyes** – should never be dull and must be free from blemishes or discharge.

2 **Ears** – mites, or other troubles, will cause head shaking.

3 **Coat** – dullness and roughness indicate poor health.
Skin – should be loose enough to move with the hand and should not feel hot.

4 **Nostrils** – membranes should be pink and moist and free from discharge.

5 **Flanks** – heavy and irregular breathing may be visible.

6 **Abdomen** – a horse with abdominal trouble will look 'tucked up', i.e., looking thinner than usual in the hind part of the abdomen.

Legs and feet

A horse's legs and feet are more likely than anything else to give him trouble. It would be remarkable for any horse to go through its life without occasional lameness. Lameness may be due to serious diseases such as navicular disease, but is much more likely to be due to strain or concussion. Check that the foot is in good condition, with no foreign bodies lodged in it and no discharge or swelling. Check also for heat in the legs and swelling around the joints. In the hind leg the hock is a weak point, in the foreleg the foot is the usual cause of lameness.

Bones of the feet

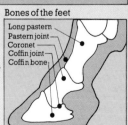

Long pastern
Pastern joint
Coronet
Coffin joint
Coffin bone

SADDLES FOR SPECIAL USES

Saddles

Jumping saddle

Show saddle

Racing saddle

Western saddle

Almost every riding discipline has evolved its own type of saddle. Some of those in regular use are shown here. **Jumping saddles** have a more forward flap and panel than the general purpose type. This is to compensate for the shorter stirrup leathers used for jumping. The knee roll is more exaggerated to give extra support to the leg. **Show saddles** are designed to show the conformation of the horse rather than aid the rider. The flap is cut straight to show the horse's shoulder and the saddle fits close to the back to achieve the illusion of an uninterrupted line. **Racing saddles** are made of very light pigskin and may weigh less than 2.2 kg (5 lb) for flat racing, and between 6.7 and 14 kg (17-30 lbs) for steeplechasing. **Western saddles,** by complete contrast, are designed to have a very deep seat so that the rider can remain comfortable all day.

There is a saddle for almost every riding activity and type of horse – as well as many traditional designs from countries with long equestrian histories. The type of saddle which is most in use for everyday riding is the general purpose saddle. A saddle has to fit the horse and be comfortable for the rider. A well fitting saddle should be well clear of the horse's withers at the pommel, and sit comfortably, neither perched nor pinching. A saddle that does not fit correctly will cause pressure and sores. All of these points must be taken into account if you are buying your own saddle.

Correct fitting
A correctly fitting saddle will sit securely on the horse's back without pinching and will be clear of the withers at the pommel.

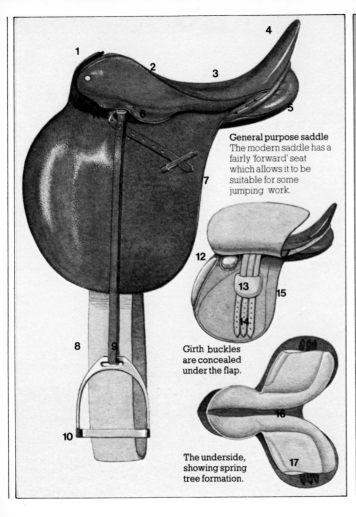

PARTS OF THE SADDLE

The modern general purpose saddle, shown on this page, is designed for the rider who wishes to hack and compete without actually specialising. It is a modified form of jumping saddle, having a deep seat to enable the rider to sit in the centre, supporting knee rolls, and is usually built on a spring tree. Some knowledge of the names given to parts of the saddle is useful when learning to ride.

General purpose saddle
The modern saddle has a fairly 'forward' seat which allows it to be suitable for some jumping work.

Girth buckles are concealed under the flap.

The underside, showing spring tree formation.

1 Pommel
2 Waist
3 Seat
4 Cantle
5 Lining
6 Skirt
7 Flap
8 Girth
9 Stirrup leathers
10 Stirrup irons
11 Stirrup bars

FLAPS UP
12 Knee roll
13 Buckle guards
14 Girth straps
15 Sweat flap

UNDERSIDE
16 Gullet
17 Panel

27

HOW TO SADDLE UP

Step one
Position the saddle on the horse's back so that the pommel arch is over, but clear of, the withers. Make sure that no part of the saddle is pressing on the horse's spine.

Step two
The girth should be attached to the other side of the saddle and folded loosely over the seat. Throw it over to the other side, collect it under the horse's belly and buckle it onto the straps on your side.

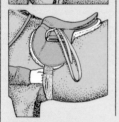

Step three
Having fastened all the starps and buckles, check the tightness of the girth by inserting your fingers between the girth and the horse. The girth should just allow the thickness of your fingers.

Removing the saddle
Before removing the saddle, run the stirrups up the leathers as far as they will go. Then unbuckle the girth, and lift the saddle from the nearside.

Bridles

The bridle is a vital part of the tack, because it provides the rider with that all-important contact with the horse's mouth through the reins and bit.

To put on a bridle, pass the reins over the horse's head whilst it is still wearing its headcollar. Then remove the headcollar, remembering for safety's sake to untie the rope if the headcollar is fastened.

Hold the headpiece of the bridle in your right hand and, standing on the near side, use your left hand to guide the bit into the horse's mouth, slipping the headpiece over the ears. Take special care not to poke the horse in the eye, pull its ears, or knock the bony prominences of the head, as this will cause the horse discomfort, possibly resulting in a future reluctance to be bridled. Make sure that the mane is lying flat under the headpiece, and pull the forelock over the browband.

Fasten the throatlash so that you can get your fist underneath it. Next fasten the noseband. A cavesson noseband lies below the cheek pieces, half-way between the corners of the mouth and the projecting cheek-bone, and you should be able to get two fingers beneath the noseband.

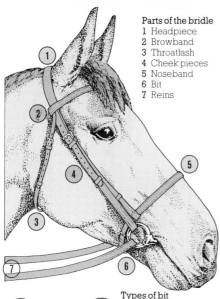

Parts of the bridle
1 Headpiece
2 Browband
3 Throatlash
4 Cheek pieces
5 Noseband
6 Bit
7 Reins

Types of bit
Most bits in common use belong to the snaffle group. These are, generally, the mildest and kindest bits. The most comfortable of all are the mullens – the rubber mullen being the easiest of all. Jointed snaffles are a little more severe, but very effective. Cheek snaffles prevent the horse pulling the bit through his mouth. They can be quite harsh, however, and must be used with care.

Mullen

Jointed snaffle

Rubber mullen

Fulmer cheek snaffle

HOW TO PUT ON A BRIDLE

Step one
Place the reins over the horse's head. If he is wearing a headcollar, leave it on until you have put the reins over the head.

Step two
While inserting the bit with your left hand, gently place the headpiece over the horse's ears. Be careful not to poke the horse in the eye or pull his ears.

Step three
Fasten the throatlash so that you can get your fist underneath it, and fasten the noseband so that you can get two fingers under it.

Removing the bridle
Undo the throatlash, loosen the noseband and, taking hold of the reins and the headpiece in your right hand, gently slip the bridle clear of the horse's head.

29

Colours

The basic colour of a horse should be characteristic of its breed. In many cases this will mean that a wide range of colours and markings will be acceptable, but there are many breeds, especially in Central Europe, which produce only one or two colours. And the Arab, a breed which is present in the ancestry of most other breeds, is usually grey, bay or chestnut. The Andalusian, an historic Spanish breed, is almost always grey.

COMMON COLOURS OF HORSES	
Bay	Brown head and body with black points. Colour variations are described as: *light bay, bright bay* and *dark bay*.
Brown	All over shade of dark brown, usually similar to dark bay.
Chestnut	Varies from a reddish to a flat golden colour. May have a blond mane and tail.
Dun	Pale brown with black points. Blue dun has a greyish tint.
Grey	An all over mixture of black and white hairs. The skin of grey horses is black.
Piebald	Irregular patches of white and black.
Skewbald	Irregular patches of white and any colour other than black.

NB When used in describing colours, *points* refers to the mane, tail and the lower part of the legs.

Grey
Grey horses are born almost black, but become lighter with age.

Palomino
Not a breed, but a colour. Most popular in the USA.

Pinto
Another American colour breed. May also be white with any other colour.

30

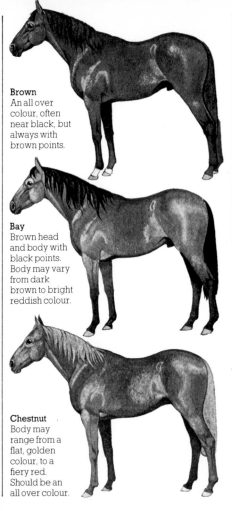

Brown
An all over colour, often near black, but always with brown points.

Bay
Brown head and body with black points. Body may vary from dark brown to bright reddish colour.

Chestnut
Body may range from a flat, golden colour, to a fiery red. Should be an all over colour.

MARKINGS

White markings on the face, legs and feet of horses are very common and not undesirable, unless they are uncharacteristic of the breed, although there are some prejudices against socks and stockings.

Face markings
Four of the most common face markings are shown on this page. You can see how confusion may arise between the blaze and the white face. The important distinction is that the white face covers the whole of the forehead and is wider than the nasal bone.

Leg and foot markings
The markings shown below are frequently encountered.
1 Stocking; 2 Sock; 3 Fetlock; 4 Heel.

1 2 3 4

Star

Blaze

Snip

White face

Anatomy of the horse

Good conformation is very important in a horse, not only because an animal that is well put together is more pleasing to the eye than its badly put together counterpart, but because faults in conformation affect the horse's ability to stay sound in work or, possibly, to survive at all.

No horse, of course, is completely perfect, but some faults in conformation are worse than others. When looking at a horse, perhaps with a view to buying it, you must weigh up the seriousness of each defect and consider how it will affect the animal's soundness or ability to perform its allotted task. A goose-rump, for instance, may not affect a horse required for jumping.

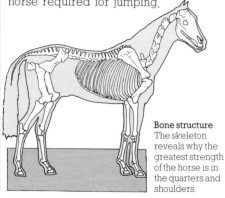

Bone structure
The skeleton reveals why the greatest strength of the horse is in the quarters and shoulders.

The illustrations below show some of the characteristics which are best avoided. Neither would make a good riding animal, and both could be prone to weakness and lameness.

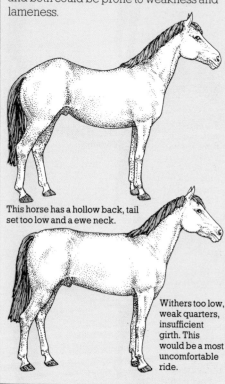

This horse has a hollow back, tail set too low and a ewe neck.

Withers too low, weak quarters, insufficient girth. This would be a most uncomfortable ride.

32

Points of the horse

1 **Ears** – small and alert.
2 **Eyes** – big but calm.
3 **Head** – carried proudly.
4 **Neck** – well-arched and showing muscle.

When making an assessment of a horse start with the head, looking for good, proud carriage and kindly, intelligent eyes – then work along the back to the rump and on to the legs and feet, checking all the points dealt with on these pages.

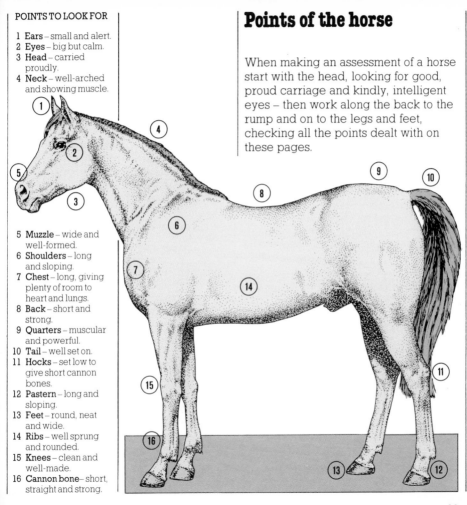

5 **Muzzle** – wide and well-formed.
6 **Shoulders** – long and sloping.
7 **Chest** – long, giving plenty of room to heart and lungs.
8 **Back** – short and strong.
9 **Quarters** – muscular and powerful.
10 **Tail** – well set on.
11 **Hocks** – set low to give short cannon bones.
12 **Pastern** – long and sloping.
13 **Feet** – round, neat and wide.
14 **Ribs** – well sprung and rounded.
15 **Knees** – clean and well-made.
16 **Cannon bone** – short, straight and strong.

33

Grooming your horse

Daily grooming stimulates the circulation, removes waste products from the skin, maintains condition and improves the appearance.

Your grooming kit should include a hoof pick, dandy brush, body brush, metal and rubber curry combs, water brush, two sponges, wisp, stable rubber, hoof oil and brush.

Horses kept at grass do not need a thorough grooming every day. It is best to leave the natural oils in their coats to provide protection from the elements. Just brush off any mud or dust and tidy the mane and tail prior to exercise.

CARING FOR TACK

Much of the tack is leather, and must be treated to keep it supple and soft. Oils are available for the untreated side of the leather, but the smooth side, the 'grain', should be cleaned with saddle soap. Never soak leather in hot water, or dry it with heat. Girths are usually made from washable materials.

GROOMING EQUIPMENT

Dandy brush

Dandy brush
A stiff brush for removing loose hair and mud from legs.

Body brush
The basic item of grooming equipment.

Body brush

Water brush
For laying the mane and tail.

Water brush

Curry comb
Used for removing hair from the body brush during grooming.

Curry combs

Hoof pick
For removing mud and debris from the feet.

Mane comb
For separating the hairs of the mane.

Hoof pick

Stable rubber
For the final polish.

Sponges
One for cleaning the dock and tail; one for the eyes, mouth and nostrils.

Mane comb

Stable rubber

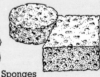
Sponges

Preparing for grooming 1

Grooming is part of the horse's daily routine – something the horse should look forward to and an important means of establishing a good relationship between handler and horse. Although grooming is a routine activity, it is not a chore. Treat it as something which is pleasant for both of you and never rush the job. Handle the grooming equipment firmly and confidently, but be gentle and sympathetic to the horse. It is not necessary to groom to show ring requirements every day, but a well turned out horse is a happy horse.

GROOMING SEQUENCE CHECK LIST

1	TIE UP THE HORSE
2	PICK OUT ALL FOUR FEET
3	REMOVE LOOSE HAIR WITH DANDY BRUSH
4	BRUSH NEAR SIDE WITH BODY BRUSH
5	BRUSH OFF SIDE WITH BODY BRUSH
6	BRUSH THE MANE
7	BRUSH THE HEAD – GENTLY
8	BRUSH THE TAIL
9	RUB WITH DAMP WISP*
10	WIPE EYES, MUZZLE AND NOSTRILS
11	WIPE DOCK REGION
12	LAY THE MANE WITH WATER BRUSH
13	OIL THE HOOVES
14	DUST WITH DAMP STABLE RUBBER

*See step-by-step sequence

ATTENDING TO THE FEET 2

Picking up the legs
To pick up the foreleg, stand by the horse's shoulder facing the tail. Run your hand down the back of the leg, and say 'up' firmly. If he does not obey, push against his shoulder to make him put his weight onto the other foot. To pick up the hind leg, stand by the horse's quarters, still facing rearwards, and run your hand down his quarters. When you reach the cannon bone, slide your hand round to the inside. As you near the foot the horse will allow you to pick up the leg. Move the leg backwards a little and rest the hoof on your knee.

Fore feet

Hind feet

Picking the feet
Using the hoof pick, remove the dirt from the foot, working from heel to toe. This avoids damage to the frog or heel.

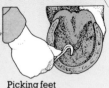
Picking feet

Oiling hooves
Regular oiling of the hooves is necessary to prevent splitting and cracking.

Oiling hooves

35

GROOMING THE BODY

- Always work from front to back – this is the way the horse's coat grows and the natural lay of the hairs.

- Use the dandy brush lightly, to remove loose hair and surface dirt. The dandy brush is very stiff and will pull and split the hairs of the mane and tail if allowed to brush through them.

- Starting at the top of the neck, just behind the ears, brush all over with the body brush. Have the curry in your right hand so that you can clean the brush every third or fourth stroke.

- Using a dampened stable rubber, rub the horse all over to remove any remaining pieces of dust and dirt.

- When you are using the grooming brushes be careful not to knock the horse in sensitive places. These are: the head, the loins and the legs.

- The **wisp**, a length of twisted and looped hay, is sometimes used after the body brush. When slightly dampened and brushed vigorously over the horse's body it has a toning and conditioning effect.

Using the body brush and curry comb

Brush off surface dirt with dandy brush

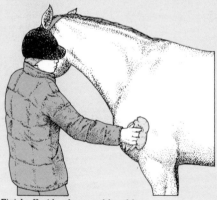

Finish off with a damp stable rubber

GROOMING THE MANE AND HEAD

4

- Do not use the dandy brush on the mane. If you do, many of the hairs will be broken off and the mane will look spare and untidy.
- Use the metal comb to separate and clean through the locks of the mane. If the mane has been pulled, you will not have much to comb. If it has not, make sure that you go right through and do not leave hairs tangled at the ends.
- Use the water brush to remove the remaining dust and make the mane lie flat.
- With a sponge that is reserved for use on the face, wipe around the eyes and the nostrils. Again, be careful not to knock the bony prominences of the head or poke the eyes.
- Some horses may try to bite you while they are being groomed. You can prevent this by holding the headcollar with a free hand, or by tying him up with a short rope. Biters are, however, least likely to try to take a lump out of you while you are sponging the face.

Sponge the eyes and mouth

Combing the mane

Laying the mane

GROOMING THE DOCK AND TAIL

5

- Groom the tail by holding it up and brushing it out piece by piece. Brush right through to the ends of the hairs.
- Remember not to use the dandy brush – if you want your horse to be left with some sort of tail.
- Use the water brush to make the tail hang straight and flat.
- Using a sponge that is reserved for the purpose, wipe around the dock area and under the tail.

Using the body brush

Equine behaviour

Those who ride, train and enjoy the horse, have cause to be grateful to the mobility of its ears because it is mainly by observing these that we determine the mood and attitude of the horse at any time. Ears flattened backwards indicate anger and are a warning to be wary; ears flopping in no general direction are a sign that the horse is dozing or bored; ears strained forward, as opposed to merely pricked, indicate that the horse can see or hear something strange and is likely to run away or shy. Pricked ears show alertness and an interest in the proceedings,

Ear signals
Pricked ears indicate alertness, but they should be mobile. A horse that listens to its rider will constantly flick back one ear. This is a good sign.

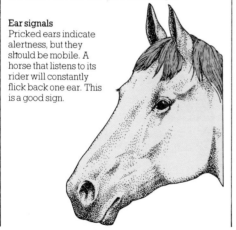

Equine memory
In the wild, the horse's defence from attack is to run, and because of this ingrained characteristic, it will shy at, or run away from, anything unfamiliar. The horse has an excellent memory and if a rider should punish it for showing fear, the problem will be compounded because the horse will remember this and connect the unfamiliar object with fear and pain. A moment's loss of temper will be remembered by the horse for a very long time and can set it back seriously in its training.

This long memory, and the gregarious nature of the horse, are exploited during training. Schooled horses are used to lend confidence to youngsters; and reward is given for obedience and progress, thus forming pleasurable associations in the mind.

For those who wish to learn more about the nature of the horse, observation of a group of horses at grass will bear a great deal of fruit. The establishment of the 'pecking order', and the daily rituals of play, rest and feeding, will give the uninitiated a greater insight into the nature of the animal which gives us so much pleasure

STABLE VICES

Lack of work, exercise, boredom or confinement may lead to a horse developing bad habits. These are usually called 'stable vices'. **Biting** and **kicking** are the worst for the handlers of such horses, but few horses are really vicious. **Kicking** may be due to irritation in the foot or boredom – seldom is it due to bad temper. **Crib-biting** is common. Such horses will bite almost any stable fitting and fill themselves with air at the same time. It has a very debilitating effect. Some horses develop the habit of violently sucking in air without biting anything, this is called **wind-sucking**. Rocking and swaying from side to side is called **weaving** and is another nervous and weakening habit.

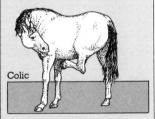

Colic

Horses that seem to kick at their flanks, and are constantly looking at them, are almost certainly suffering from colic.

Rearing

Kicking

Napping

BAD HABITS

Usually, bad behaviour is due to bad handling, not only through maltreatment, but also through poor training. **Bucking** is not all that common, although high spirited horses are sometimes accused of it. A genuine buck is an attempt to unseat the rider and must be punished. It may, however, owe its origins to the use of the whip – so be careful. **Rearing** is dangerous, to horse and rider. Habitual rearing is intolerable. Sometimes it is caused by fear or pain and may not be repeated if the cause is removed, but rearing caused by previous bad handling is incurable. **Shying** and **bolting** are usually caused by sudden fear, or too sharp a reaction by the rider to something unexpected. Bolters, however, may run away without apparent reason. Avoid them if you can. **Napping** is deliberate disobedience or wilfullness. It can be cured but it takes time.

The importance of good riding instruction

The importance of good riding instruction cannot be overstressed. Bad habits formed in the early stages of learning to ride are difficult to overcome, and no real progress will be made until they are ironed-out. This obviously takes time and money, and need never be necessary if the riding establishment at which you choose to take your lessons is selected with care.

The first stipulation is to make your choice only from establishments approved either by your national equestrian society or an association of riding schools. Most run stringent approvals schemes and you can at least be sure that you will ride a well-fed suitable horse or pony with well-fitting tack and have your lessons with a qualified instructor.

However, even the standard of approved centres varies and, although it may cost you a little more, it is worth delving deep into your pocket and going to the very best your area can offer.

A well-run yard will be distinguished by its well-swept, tidy appearance, neatly turned-out staff, alert, happy horses, clean stables and tack, and a general air of efficiency and order.

Riding schools

Almost all approved riding instruction takes place in a *manège,* (see page 42) and conforms to an internationally recognised set of exercises and techniques. To the newcomer, riding school instruction may seem elaborate and unnecessary, but, unless you have had your own ponies since childhood, it is probably the only way to make rapid progress – especially if your riding is limited to one session per week.

It is a good idea when choosing a riding school – especially one for a child – to watch one or two lessons in progress before committing to it. Some riding schools are inclined to overbook their courses and overstress their instructors. In these circumstances, it can be very difficult for new riders, including adults, to respond to instruction quickly enough. Consequently, too many intelligent, and potentially able, riders are made to feel inadequate. This in no way lessens the need for good instruction – it simply means that you must be careful to ensure that you are getting it. Remember that a good rider is patient, willing to learn and sympathetic to the horse; a good instructor is patient and sympathetic with pupils.

RIDING INSTRUCTION IN THE U.K.

Most countries run broadly similar schemes for the training and approval of instructors – who come in all shapes, sizes and degrees of qualification. The British Horse Society examinations structure runs from the British Horse Society Assistant Instructor's examination (B.H.S.A.I.) through the British Horse Society Intermediate Instructor's examination (B.H.S.I.I.) to the British Horse Society Instructor's examination (B.H.S.I.), culminating in the Fellowship of the British Horse Society (F.B.H.S.) to which high standard very few attain.

Obviously a centre run by an F.B.H.S. or B.H.S.I. will offer instruction to a higher level than that run by a B.H.S.A.I. This doesn't mean, however, that a B.H.S.A.I. is not well enough qualified to teach you. In all likelihood you will be instructed by a B.H.S.A.I. initially, whichever school you choose, but a centre run by a B.H.S.I. or F.B.H.S. does offer you the opportunity to progress further when *you* reach B.H.S.A.I. standard.

Unless you are prepared to pay extra for private lessons, you will find that most rides consist of two to six riders.

Riding in a manège

Riding in a manège for the first time can be confusing, so it is as well to learn the positions of the markers before your first lesson. The markers are **A, K, E, H, C, M, B** and **F**, and in order to familiarise yourself with them it helps to memorise a rhyme, i.e., **A**ll **K**ing **E**dward's **H**orses **C**all **M**e **B**lessed **F**ool.

The rider leading the ride is addressed as 'leading file' and is responsible for setting and maintaining pace. The ride will be either on the left rein, where the riders' left arms are on the inside, or on the right rein, where the riders' right arms are on the inside. At all times, unless instructed to the contrary, you should carry your whip in your inside hand.

Not all horses move at the same speed, particularly when ridden by novices, so some variation in the distances between the members of the ride is bound to occur. You should maintain half a horse's length (or four feet) between your horse and the horse in front. Should you become left behind, correct your distance by cutting the corners, not by increasing pace. If you get too close to the preceding horse, make a half-circle and turn away.

MANÈGE EXERCISES

Most exercises in the manège involve riding circles, making diagonal movements across the school in order to change the rein and riding from one marker to another. The leaving and rejoining of markers must be exact.

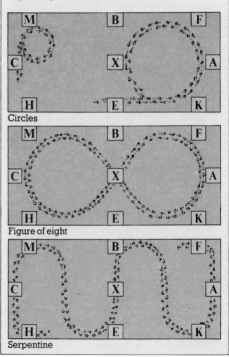

Circles

Figure of eight

Serpentine

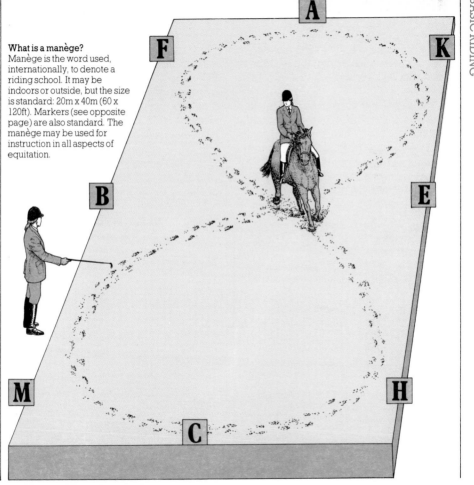

What is a manège?
Manège is the word used, internationally, to denote a riding school. It may be indoors or outside, but the size is standard: 20m x 40m (60 x 120ft). Markers (see opposite page) are also standard. The manège may be used for instruction in all aspects of equitation.

Riding clothes

Riding clothes are designed, not only to give a smart and workmanlike appearance, but also for the safety and comfort of the rider.

The *hard hat* is the most vital item and it is important that it fits correctly, meaning that it should stay in place even if you are hurtling headfirst to the ground! Strictly speaking, chin straps, though disliked by most for reasons of vanity, should be used, and they can make all the difference.

WINTER RIDING CLOTHES

Cold weather kit
It must be accepted that, during cold weather, a stylish turn-out is less important than keeping warm. A cold rider is unlikely to be a very effective one. Quilted waistcoats and anoraks, worn over sweaters are ideal for winter riding. This is a combination which allows considerable freedom of movement as well as giving good insulation. Gloves, of course, are standard items.

The second item of riding kit that you cannot do without is a pair of *boots*. Whether these are leather top boots, rubber riding boots or jodhpur boots, they shouldn't have a thick, or half, sole, because this might result in your foot becoming caught in the stirrup should you fall. For the same reason, ordinary shoes and tennis shoes are out.

Jodhpurs or breeches are also important. Jeans do not give your leg adequate protection and will allow the stirrup leathers to pinch your calves.

Ideally, a *shirt* and *tie* looks very smart, but a *sweater*, open-necked blouse or T-shirt will suffice for hacking. You can wear either a *hacking jacket* or a *quilted anorak*, and during cold weather a *quilted waistcoat*.

You should wear *gloves* all the time, summer and winter. You may not like the idea of gloves in the summer, but they are a great help when the reins are sticky. Once you are used to wearing them, you'll never want to ride without them.

To complete your outfit, you should carry a *stick* or *whip* which, even if you never have cause to use it on your horse, is useful for poking branches and brambles out of the way!

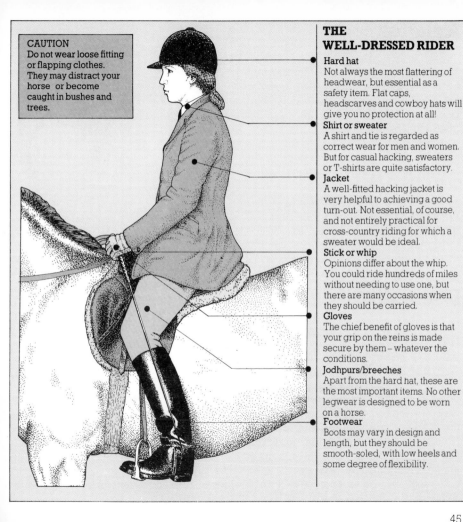

THE WELL-DRESSED RIDER

Hard hat
Not always the most flattering of headwear, but essential as a safety item. Flat caps, headscarves and cowboy hats will give you no protection at all!

Shirt or sweater
A shirt and tie is regarded as correct wear for men and women. But for casual hacking, sweaters or T-shirts are quite satisfactory.

Jacket
A well-fitted hacking jacket is very helpful to achieving a good turn-out. Not essential, of course, and not entirely practical for cross-country riding for which a sweater would be ideal.

Stick or whip
Opinions differ about the whip. You could ride hundreds of miles without needing to use one, but there are many occasions when they should be carried.

Gloves
The chief benefit of gloves is that your grip on the reins is made secure by them – whatever the conditions.

Jodhpurs/breeches
Apart from the hard hat, these are the most important items. No other legwear is designed to be worn on a horse.

Footwear
Boots may vary in design and length, but they should be smooth-soled, with low heels and some degree of flexibility.

45

Mounting

Mounting is sometimes difficult at first. Indeed, it can be quite a feat for some experienced riders! Certainly, it helps to be fit and light on one's feet – but this goes for all aspects of riding.

Remember to keep the reins and stick in your left hand, keeping the reins fairly short. Allow too much rein to your horse and he may try to walk away while you mount. Do not land heavily in the saddle – you could quite easily hurt the animal's back, and you will certainly not endear yourself to him.

Step one
Stand facing the tail, with the reins and stick in your left hand. Grasp the neck or mane with your left hand and place your left foot in the stirrup.

Step two
Placing your right hand on the saddle (not on the cantle), spring up – taking most of your weight with your right arm.

Dismounting

Both dismounting and mounting are correctly performed only on the near side (the horse's left). Dismounting is unquestionably easier but is too often done in a rather sloppy manner. Try always to land clear of the horse and avoid slithering down the animal's side. Never, on any account, try to spring from the saddle by using the stirrup as a platform. You may, too easily, leave your foot in the stirrup and turn a somersault on the way down.

Step one
Take both feet out of the irons, put the reins and stick into your left hand and place your right hand on the pommel.

Step two
Lean forward, taking the weight on your hands, and swing your right leg over, clear of the quarters.

46

Step three
Swing your right leg up and *clear* of the horse's back. It is vital not to brush his back or kick his quarters during this movement.

Step four
Settle yourself *gently* into the saddle, put your right foot into the stirrup iron, and take up the reins with both hands.

Step three
When your right leg is clear of the horse, twist slightly so that you land facing the same way as the horse.

Step four
Take the reins in both hands, as shown above, keeping the stick in your left hand. This is the correct leading position.

CHECK GIRTHS AND STIRRUPS

Before mounting you must check your girth and pull down your stirrups. Don't make the mistake of doing the girth up uncomfortably tight. You should be able to get your hand under the girth. After you have tightened it lift the horse's foreleg and pull it forward to ease out any wrinkles in the skin that might pinch.

Adjusting girth *(left)*
When in the saddle, adjust by lifting the flap and pulling the girth straps upwards.

Checking stirrups *(below)*
Before mounting, check the length of stirrups by measuring against your arm. As a rough guide, the stirrup bar should reach your armpit.

47

The hands and the reins

Sympathetic, responsive hands are of vital importance to every rider. The horse begins its training with a soft, sensitive mouth, and it is by abuse from over-strong hands that hard mouths and evasions are formed.

The reins should be held in both hands, and pass between the little and third finger, and between the thumb and first finger. The thumb should be on top and the spare loop of rein should be allowed to fall down the horse's shoulder, lying underneath the length of rein running from the bit to the hand so as not to interfere with its use. For the same reason the reins should lie flat with no twists. The hands should be held at least four inches apart and of a length to allow the elbow to be in front of the hip.

As the horse moves, its head nods and the hands must follow this movement so as not to pull or jog at the mouth and ruin its sensitivity. It is important, though, that the hands do not move more than is necessary and, apart from following and allowing this natural movement, the rider should maintain a still hand.

The rider's position in the saddle can be described with the help of several straight lines, and these will be explained on the following page. One of these lines, however, concerns the hands the rider should see a straight line from the bit, along the rein, through the wrist to the elbow.

The hands should be independent of the seat at all times, and the rider should never use them to hold on with. The rider should use the hands in conjunction with the seat and legs, and not alone. It must be remembered that it is the strong and heavy use of the hand that produces a strong and heavy horse, and a light, sympathetic hand that produces a light, responsive horse.

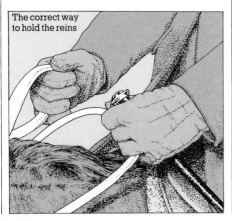

The correct way to hold the reins

Maintaining contact

You will often hear references to 'contact' during the course of riding instruction. A good contact is one in which the rider, at all paces, holds the reins in the correct manner and at the correct length. The ideal length is one which enables the horse to be aware of the rider's hands and the rider to be in touch with the horse's mouth, without any pulling or discomfort. A good contact is important at all times, but particularly during transitions (change of pace).

COMMON FAULTS

Reins too far apart

Spare rein on wrong side

Incorrect reins
Holding the reins too far apart, *left*, is an error which is easily corrected. It is so difficult to achieve any degree of control in this way that only absolute beginners are guilty – usually! Turning the thumbs down and carrying the spare rein on the wrong side, *left*, may be a long term bad habit if not corrected in the early stages. If the reins are too loose, *below*, the rider has no contact at all with the horse's mouth.

Example of good contact.

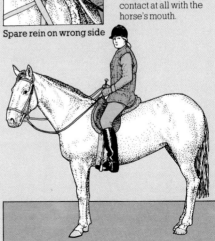

Reins too loose

49

The seat

An independent seat is maintained by balance, suppleness and anticipation. For the experienced rider grip will play a part, but a novice told to grip will stiffen the knee and thigh, turn out the toes, and grip with the calf, consequently forcing the seat upwards and out of the saddle.

The rider must sit in the central and lowest part of the saddle, with the upper body upright without being stiff, and should look between the horse's ears. Weight should be felt on the rider's seatbones, and the thigh and knee should be close to the saddle to form a natural downwards and inwards grip. The knee and ankle must be supple without any stiffness. A relaxed

THE CORRECT SEAT

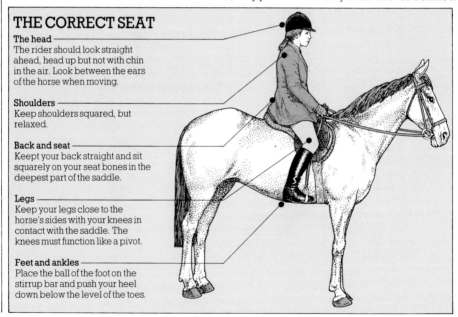

The head
The rider should look straight ahead, head up but not with chin in the air. Look between the ears of the horse when moving.

Shoulders
Keep shoulders squared, but relaxed.

Back and seat
Keep your back straight and sit squarely on your seat bones in the deepest part of the saddle.

Legs
Keep your legs close to the horse's sides with your knees in contact with the saddle. The knees must function like a pivot.

Feet and ankles
Place the ball of the foot on the stirrup bar and push your heel down below the level of the toes.

knee will cause the lower leg to come naturally back into contact with the horse's sides and the stirrup leather should hang vertically.

The rider's ankle acts as a shock absorber and must therefore be supple. The heels should be lower than the toes, which should point forward turning out *very* slightly, and the ball of the foot should rest in the stirrup.

One of the three straight lines which you should be able to observe in a rider sitting correctly was described in the preceding pages. Of the other two, one should run from the shoulder through the hip to the heel, and the other down the seam of the riding cap, along the spine and the seam of the jodhpurs, and down the stitching on the back of the saddle.

The rider's arms should hang naturally, with the elbows bent and touching the sides softly.

The correct position will, of course, feel strange at first, but practice combined with suppling exercises will strengthen the relevant muscles. The rider should remain supple and light, sitting deep in the saddle, at the same time drawing back the shoulder blades and thinking tall.

THE INCORRECT SEAT

The examples shown below are exaggerated versions of common faults. Although exaggerated, they are not unusual and many riders demonstrate them to a greater or lesser extent. In these examples, the rider will not be in control.

Rider slumped forward, heels too far back. Rider will be tense and unbalanced.

Rider leaning back: poor control with legs and a tendency to pull horse's mouth.

Lengthening & shortening stirrups & reins

Over-long stirrup leathers will weaken the rider's seat, whereas leathers too short will increase the rider's security but will also push the seat too far back in the saddle and reduce the use of the legs. It is important, therefore, that the leathers are adjusted carefully.

Most beginners ride with their leathers too short, but further lessons and work without stirrups will help the rider to work down into the saddle.

The method of measuring the leathers before mounting is shown on page 47. To alter the length of your stirrups when mounted, put your reins and whip into the opposite hand, *keep both feet in the stirrups*, and alter the leather with one hand. It takes a little practice and, depending on the size of your leg, you may need to lift your thigh to do it.

To shorten your reins, take the opposite rein between the thumb and forefinger and slide the free hand down the rein, reversing the process for the other rein. To lengthen the reins, allow them to slide through your fingers to the required length. Never lengthen or shorten your reins by fiddling your fingers along the rein, as this destroys your contact with the horse's mouth.

ADJUSTING THE STIRRUPS

When in the saddle, the stirrups can be adjusted quite easily by lifting the skirt of the saddle and pulling the stirrup leather through the buckle.

Checking length
When mounted, the rider's toe should be just about level with the stirrup bar when the leg is put into a comfortable 'riding' position. The heel should be slightly lower, but the rider should not feel that his toe is being pushed up by the stirrup bar.

HOW TO ADJUST THE REINS

Lengthening and shortening the reins are manoeuvres which must be carried out smoothly and with the minimum of fuss. Contact must be maintained at all times, so do not allow the reins to slip away from you when changing your grip.

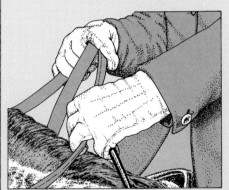

Shortening the reins
To shorten the left rein, for example, grip the rein just above your left hand with the thumb and forefinger of your right hand and pull the reins through to the required length. Take a proper grip with your left hand and repeat the process for the right rein.

COMMON FAULTS

Stirrups too long: rider cannot apply heel to girth.

Stirrups too short: rider will be unbalanced and have poor control.

53

The aids

Aids are the commands by which the rider makes known his wishes to the horse. There are two types of aid, natural and artificial, the former being the hands, legs, voice and body, and the latter whips, spurs and martingales.

Aids should be applied lightly, yet definitely, so that the horse receives a clear message from its rider. Young horses often require the aids to be exaggerated, but as a horse progresses in its training the aids will become more and more discreet.

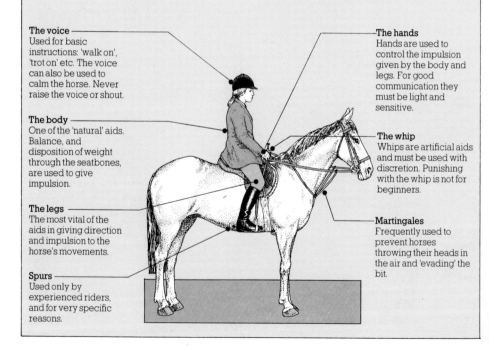

The voice
Used for basic instructions: 'walk on', 'trot on' etc. The voice can also be used to calm the horse. Never raise the voice or shout.

The body
One of the 'natural' aids. Balance, and disposition of weight through the seatbones, are used to give impulsion.

The legs
The most vital of the aids in giving direction and impulsion to the horse's movements.

Spurs
Used only by experienced riders, and for very specific reasons.

The hands
Hands are used to control the impulsion given by the body and legs. For good communication they must be light and sensitive.

The whip
Whips are artificial aids and must be used with discretion. Punishing with the whip is not for beginners.

Martingales
Frequently used to prevent horses throwing their heads in the air and 'evading' the bit.

Riding on the lunge

Working a rider on the lunge assists in developing balance, an independent seat and hands, 'feel', and deepness in the saddle. Lunge lessons should always be of short duration, up to a maximum of half an hour, so as not to tire the rider and encourage resultant stiffness.

In a lungeing lesson the instructor controls the horse whilst the rider works without reins or stirrups, the reins being knotted on the horse's neck with the knot falling to the inside, and the stirrups crossed over the horse's shoulders.

A horse tacked up correctly for lungeing should be wearing a snaffle bridle (with reins) under a lungeing cavesson, and adjustable side reins running from the bit to the girth straps. The lungeing rein should be attached to the front ring of the cavesson. If a Wells cavesson is used, the noseband should be taken off the bridle because the nosepiece of this lungeing cavesson fastens under the bit in the same way as a drop noseband. The horse should wear brushing boots on all four legs for protection, and the instructor should carry a lungeing whip.

Various exercises, some of which will be described on the following page, are performed, mainly while the horse is in trot, although absolute beginners will also work in walk. The trot must be even and rhythmical but, at the same time, fairly lively. An idle trot is too easy to sit to and the rider will learn nothing.

A rider dressing for a lunge lesson must put on a pair of gloves, but might find that leaving off a jacket or a jumper is a good idea. It can be hot work!

The lungeing lesson
Lungeing can be used to train horses or riders. It improves the rider's balance and seat.

EXERCISES ON THE LUNGE

There are a great variety of exercises for the rider to perform on the lunge. All will become easier with practice, although they will feel strange and difficult to begin with. Some are performed only at halt, such as clapping the heels above the croup, but most are performed at walk and trot. At the beginning of a lesson the rider should be allowed to walk and trot a few circuits with reins and stirrups, and when these are taken away the rider should, at first, hold onto the front of the saddle with both hands. All exercises should be performed on both reins. As the series of exercises progresses, the instructor will continually correct the rider's position. You will be surprised to see how, the moment you perform an arm or body exercise, a leg slides out of the correct position! Your aim is to make your arms, legs and seat independent of movement in other parts. On these pages are a selection of exercises designed to develop suppleness, muscle and balance.

1. Arms outstretched

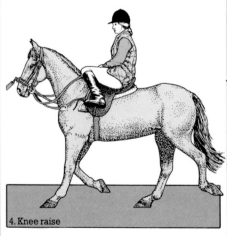

4. Knee raise

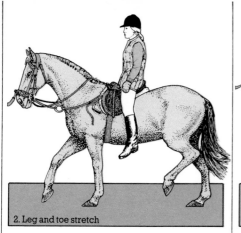

2. Leg and toe stretch

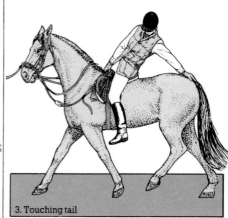

3. Touching tail

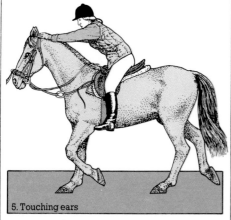

5. Touching ears

6. Leg raise

EXERCISES ON PAGES 56-59

1. Riding with **arms outstretched,** especially when swinging them from side to front, develops grip.
2. **Leg and toe stretching** is used to supple the ankles and make the rider sit deep in the saddle.
3. **Touching the tail,** especially at the trot, is an excellent exercise for balance.
4. **Raising the knees,** like a jockey, encourages the rider to use seat bones.
5. **Touching the horse's ears** is another exercise for grip and balance.
6. The sideways **leg raise** is a strenuous exercise, but very effective in suppling the hips and strengthening the thighs.
7. **Arm circling,** like arm swinging, is good for balance.
8. **Touching the toes** is easier than it looks; encourages the rider to ride with the legs.
9. **Leaning back in the saddle** will develop a relaxed, but firm, seat.
10. **Shoulder circling** encourages the rider to keep a straight back and relaxed arms.
11. **Touching toes with the opposite hand** is more difficult than 8, but more beneficial.
12. **The leg swing** is not for your first experience of lungeing, but is a great confidence builder.

7. Arm circling

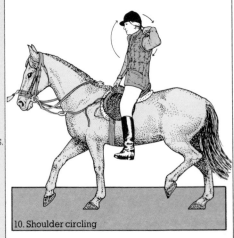

10. Shoulder circling

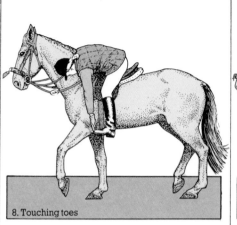

8. Touching toes

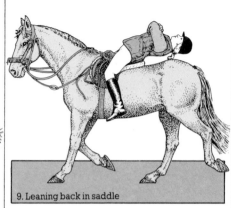

9. Leaning back in saddle

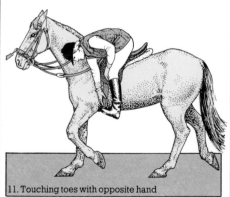

11. Touching toes with opposite hand

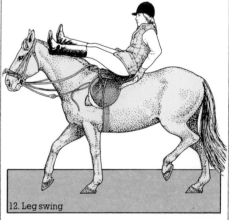

12. Leg swing

The walk

The walk is a pace of four-time with a distinctly-marked cadence, and it is at this pace that the beginner becomes familiar with riding forward, using the markers, performing turns and circles, halting, and lengthening and shortening the reins.

In walk the rider must sit upright with the weight evenly distributed on the seatbones and look in the direction of travel, avoiding any tendency to lean forward.

The horse has a natural, swinging rhythm in walk, and the rider's body must quietly follow this without changing position. The hands must also follow the movement without being in any way exaggerated.

To ask for walk from halt the rider should close both legs, straighten the spine and ease the hands, although a contact must be maintained with the horse's mouth. As soon as the horse responds by moving forward, the leg aid can be eased and used as necessary to maintain the walk.

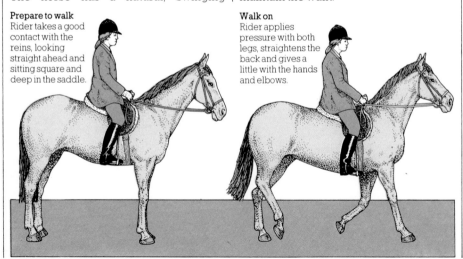

Prepare to walk
Rider takes a good contact with the reins, looking straight ahead and sitting square and deep in the saddle.

Walk on
Rider applies pressure with both legs, straightens the back and gives a little with the hands and elbows.

Turns and circles

In turns and circles the rider uses the diagonal aids, and it must be remembered that a leg aid always precedes a hand aid because the horse is always worked from back to front, never vice versa.

To turn right, therefore, the rider should be using both legs to ask the horse to go forward. The right hand is carried outwards leading the horse into a gentle turn. This open rein aid will, as the rider progresses, give way to a more discreet aid, applied without the necessity of carrying out the hand. The left hand must allow the horse to bend to the right without losing the contact. At the same time, the rider's left leg should be applied behind the girth in order to control the hindquarters and keep the hindfeet following the forefeet. The forward movement is maintained by the right leg applied on the girth. In all turns and circles the horse must bend in the body, not just in the neck.

It may appear somewhat mystifying to beginners that experienced riders can instruct their horses to turn without giving any obvious instructions. This is one of the subleties of riding which become second nature with practice.

HOW TO TURN

Many beginners are confused by the use of the word 'diagonal' with reference to the aids. In practice, this simply means that you lead with the inside rein (the side to which the horse will turn), using the inside leg to maintain impulsion, supporting the movement with the outside rein and leg.

The hands
The leading hand carries the rein outwards slightly in the direction of the turn, while the other hand moves forward a little to allow for the shift in the rein. Maintain contact throughout the action.

The legs
The inside leg is applied to the girth to keep the horse going forward, while the opposite leg is applied behind the girth to prevent the hindquarters from swinging outwards. Keep the legs in these positions until the turn has been completed.

Halting & transitions

The rider asks for halt by closing both legs, sitting deep, yet tall, in the saddle, and bringing the horse into a still hand. Never attempt to ask for a halt by use of the hands alone, because this results in a loss of control of the hindquarters which will swing out, resulting in a ragged, untidy transition.

Any change of pace or speed, or transition, should be precise, smooth and progressive. Downward transitions (where the horse comes from a faster pace into a slower pace) are more difficult to perfect than upwards transitions (where the horse moves into a faster pace from a slower pace).

When riding in a manège it is important to ride accurately to the markers. If instructed, for instance, to change the rein across the diagonal from H to F the horse must leave the track precisely at H and rejoin it precisely at F. A yard either side is not good enough. If asked to halt at a marker, the rider should plan the movement so that when the horse is stationary it is the rider who is level with the marker.

Halting
When the rider asks for a halt by closing the legs, the effect is one of driving the horse forward into hands that will not give. The pressure of the legs is the recognised signal for moving forward, but the resistance of the hands countermands this instruction and the horse stops. Resistance is achieved, simply, by closing the fingers firmly, never by pulling.

The correct position at halt

Riding without stirrups

Work without stirrups encourages a deeper seat, supples the limbs and body, and improves balance and confidence. It should be introduced to a lesson after horse and rider have warmed-up, and the horse is settled.

When instructed to 'quit and cross your stirrups' the rider should slide both feet from the stirrups and cross the leathers over the horse's shoulders in front of the saddle. The off-side stirrup is always crossed first so that should the rider need to dismount for any reason, the near-side stirrup will be easily obtainable for mounting again.

Most work without stirrups is performed at sitting trot and the rider may be asked to perform exercises such as putting the reins and stick into the outside hand and circling the inside arm backwards. Exercises of this nature are designed to aid independence of the limbs and body. Despite the circling arm both legs *should* remain in the correct position!

More advanced riders may also be asked to do a little rising trot without stirrups, although this will be too strenuous for beginners.

It is important that only short periods of time are spent riding without stirrups, because tired muscles will force the rider to adopt an incorrect position in order to relieve them.

When the stirrups are taken back, the rider will often want to let them down a hole or two because the work without stirrups has had its desired effect of bringing the rider deeper into the saddle.

Crossed stirrups
The stirrups should always be crossed so that the nearside (left) stirrup is the first to be reclaimed. Riding without stirrups is easier than it looks, because it forces the rider deeper into the saddle.

The trot

The trot is a pace of two-time, the horse's legs moving in diagonal pairs, and can be ridden either by sitting or rising.

During **sitting trot** the rider remains in closer contact with the horse because the seat doesn't leave the saddle, and will find control of the hindquarters more complete. For the beginner, sitting trot should be attempted for short periods only, as it is strenuous for undeveloped muscles.

Rising trot is easier for both horse and rider. The natural rhythm and spring of the trot pushes the rider out of the saddle on one beat, and the rider then allows the seat to return quietly to the saddle on the next beat.

As mentioned before, in trot the horse's legs move in two diagonal pairs, the near-fore and the off-hind forming the left diagonal, and the off-fore and near-hind the right diagonal. A rider performing rising trot in a manège or on a circle (including on the lunge) should ride on the outside diagonal, i.e., on the right diagonal when on the left rein, and vice versa. This means that the seat of the rider trotting on the left rein should return to the saddle as the off-fore and near-hind come to the ground. Eventually the rider will be able to identify the correct diagonal by feel, but at first it may be necessary to watch the outside shoulder.

The diagonal should be changed

The trot
This is a two-beat pace in which the opposite fore and hind feet (off-fore, near hind) strike the ground together. The *ordinary* trot is a natural pace for the horse, but the *collected* trot, which is a slow and springy action, is not. The *extended* trot needs a longer and faster stride, and is a very tiring pace.

when the rein is altered, and at intervals when out hacking, and the rider does this by sitting for one extra beat. To ask a horse to trot from walk the rider should apply pressure with both calves, and ease the reins slightly.

Rising trot

The rider moves with the beat of the horse's gait. Rising out of the saddle as one diagonal pair of legs move forward, and returning to the saddle as the opposite diagonal comes forward. This is a technique learned by 'feel'.

The canter

Despite the obvious temptation, canter, which is a three-time pace with a rocking rhythm, must never be attempted until the rider is reasonably proficient at walk and trot.

In order to help balance the horse on turns and circles, the rider should ask it to canter with the inside foreleg leading. To ask for canter from trot the rider should establish a steady, regular trot rhythm and take sitting trot. As the horse comes into a corner of the manège the rider should apply the outside leg behind the girth and the inside leg on the girth, at the same time maintaining a steady contact and a slight bend to the inside. This bend, and the use of a corner or circle for the transition, aids the horse in striking off with the inside lead as requested, although as the rider advances it will be possible to obtain the desired lead whilst the horse is working on the straight.

In canter the rider must sit upright, without being rigid or stiff, allowing the upper body to give with the rocking rhythm, and the seat should not leave the saddle. As in all paces the weight must be evenly distributed on both seat bones and the rider must not lean to the inside. Whenever working in a manège, or on a circle, the rider should look in the direction of travel.

The rider should never look down the horse's shoulder in order to discover

How a horse canters
The canter is a three beat pace. This means that only one movement in three is by a diagonal pair of legs. The result is a swinging, or rocking, gait. Horses canter at greatly varying speeds: the *ordinary* canter should be quite slow, but the *extended* canter can be not far short of a gallop.

which canter lead it has taken, but should judge this by feel. It is also very important to establish a steady, regular trot, as the horse will find it impossible to strike off if allowed to trot too quickly.

To bring the horse back into trot from canter the rider should keep the legs close to the horse's sides, brace the back slightly and send the horse forward into a resisting hand. In this way the horse should make a smooth downwards transition, rather than falling raggedly head-first into a clumsy trot.

In all downward transitions the rider must guard against falling forward as the horse decreases pace.

Correct cantering position
The rider must sit well into the saddle, remaining upright but swaying forward and back with the tempo of the gait. Allow the hands to give with the stretching of the horse's neck.

About this stage

The first stage of basic instruction has included all of the elementary riding school work, but the later phases of a course of instruction would usually involve some hacking – under supervision. Riding solo along roads and in open countryside should not be attempted until some advanced work has been done in the school.

Although this is described as an advanced stage, there are elements within it which are valuable to all riders. You may not want to show your horse or take part in dressage tests, but every rider wants to be able to ride out on his own, and most want to be able to jump. Indeed, basic training is not completed without some jumping instruction.

Jumping, which is approached via exercises over trotting poles and cavaletti (small jumps, the height of which can be adjusted by turning over the cross-shaped uprights), is an essential part of learning to ride. Nobody should think himself a rider unless he can cope with jumps of a moderate size.

On the other hand, jumping is not something that should be attempted until a reasonable standard of proficiency at the elementary work is reached. But, remember, you never stop learning to ride; moving on to more advanced work does not mean that you should stop doing your basic exercises.

This section also deals with preparations for showing your horse or pony. This may only be of practical use to a small percentage of readers, but it is useful to know what is expected of horses and riders in the show ring.

Hacking

Hacking should not be attempted until the rider is well able to control the horse at walk, trot and canter, and even then it is wise to be accompanied by an experienced rider. It is a mistake to hack out too soon and there is no more uncomfortable sight than a string of horses and ponies trotting along with their novice riders bouncing uncomfortably hither and thither, bringing pleasure neither to themselves or their mounts. On the other hand, for the capable rider, there is no finer way to enjoy the countryside than from the back of a horse.

Unfortunately, most riders have occasion to use the roads and, due to the great volume of traffic on today's roads and the unfamiliarity of many drivers with the nature of the horse, it is necessary to exercise extreme caution. Major roads should be avoided whenever possible, and vigilance maintained the whole time for approaching traffic and other hazards. Even a horse that is traffic-proof might shy at something in the verge or on the pavement, and step into the path of a passing car. Common everyday occurrences, such a dog in a garden, or somebody opening a gate, can be sufficient to cause trouble. It is also important to remember to thank any motorist who does give way

or slow down. If the reins and stick are fully occupying the hands, a nod and a smile will do!

Consideration to other riders is also important. Never approach another rider at trot, canter or gallop, but return to walk. Any rider on a young or flighty horse on a windy day will appreciate the gesture, and who knows when the positions may be reversed!

Hacking provides the ideal opportunity for the rider to jump small logs and ditches, and this is great fun, as well as being excellent practice for both rider and horse.

An introduction to jumping

Jumping consists of four stages, the approach, the take-off, the period of suspension, and the landing.

When jumping, the rider uses a shorter length of stirrup and the weight is taken on the knee and thigh and down into the heel. The rider must look up in the direction of travel, with the back supple yet straight and the shoulders forward. The seat bones should come just out of the saddle over the fence, and the hands must allow for, and follow, the movement.

The straight line from the horse's mouth, along the reins, and through the wrist to the elbow, should be maintained.

Basic exercises

The first exercise consists of walking over a single heavy pole on the ground. The rider should adopt the jumping position, paying particular attention to staying in balance with the horse without using the hands as an anchor. A second pole can be introduced around four-and-a-half to five-and-a-half feet away from the first.

When the rider is competent at staying in balance at walk, the exercise can be attempted in rising trot, the number of poles in use gradually being increased to six, and the exercise being ridden on both reins and from both directions.

FOUR STAGES OF JUMPING

1 The approach
The horse gathers its hocks under its quarters and stretches its neck.

2 Take-off
Rider shifts weight forward and out of the saddle.

3 Mid-jump
Rider still clear of saddle, legs flexed, hands forward and low.

Apart from accustoming the rider to the feel of the jumping position, this work over poles also teaches both horse and rider the value of a straight approach, which is of vital importance and the foundation of successful jumping.

As a progression from poles to small fences, a cavalletti at its lowest height can be placed around 9–10 feet away from the last trotting pole, and as the rider becomes more competent the cavalletti can be put to its full height, and eventually the trotting poles replaced with other cavalletti to form combinations or a grid.

4 The landing
Rider moves back into the saddle to keep weight off the forehand.

POLES AND CAVALLETTI

The introduction to jumping will always be via trotting poles and cavalletti.

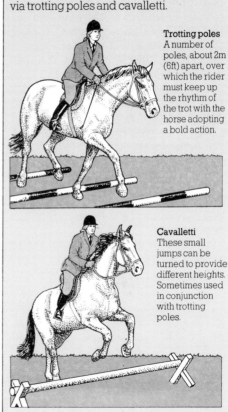

Trotting poles
A number of poles, about 2m (6ft) apart, over which the rider must keep up the rhythm of the trot with the horse adopting a bold action.

Cavalletti
These small jumps can be turned to provide different heights. Sometimes used in conjunction with trotting poles.

Further jumping

As the rider becomes more proficient over trotting poles and cavalletti, small fences, around two feet high and two feet wide, can be introduced. To jump these the horse will need to round its back more, which will give the rider more of a feel of what jumping is all about. The rider, in turn, will need to give more with the hands to accommodate this extra movement.

Small fences with 18 feet, or one canter stride, between them will introduce the rider to combinations. The difficulty here is that the rider must sit up again between fences, and at first this will be far from easy, although the grid work will have formed a very useful introduction.

At all times the rider must remember to form a straight approach to fences,

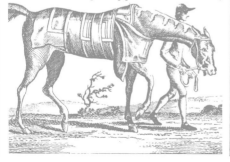

and to look at the next fence to be jumped, especially when short, simple courses are introduced.

An inexperienced rider should always be mounted on an experienced horse, because the ability to see a stride and, ultimately, to adjust the stride, are qualities gained only by time and practice, and an experienced horse will look after the novice rider.

When riding a small course the rider should bring the horse back into trot in the corners, so that changes of direction can be accomplished in balance and without undue haste.

When approaching a fence the rider's legs must be used quietly, yet firmly, in rhythm with the stride. Enormous thumps and verbal encouragement are quite unnecessary, and won't help at all.

At this early stage it is more important to introduce width to the fences than height, and before any jumping commences both horse and rider must be warmed up. Asking a horse to jump 'cold' is asking for mistakes. It must also be remembered that jumping is 90% flat work, and only a small part of each lesson should be devoted to jumping at this stage.

MORE ADVANCED JUMPING

Most riders have little intention of racing or point-to-pointing, so jumping at speed is not greatly relevant. But jumping obstacles in open country, whether for fun or in the course of organised cross-country riding, is something which is within the scope of almost every rider.

Correct jumping seat

In the picture below, the rider adopts a more forward position than usual, but achieves this by bending only from the hips. The hands are forward and low. Stirrup leathers are a couple of holes shorter than usual to bring more of the thigh into contact with the saddle.

TYPES OF JUMP

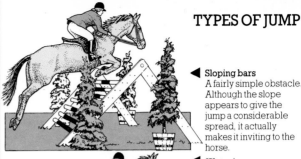

◀ **Sloping bars**
A fairly simple obstacle. Although the slope appears to give the jump a considerable spread, it actually makes it inviting to the horse.

◀ **Water jump**
In international competitions the water can be up to 5m (16ft) wide! In minor events, however, they are not so formidable. Many horses fault at the water jump because their riders send them into the jump too fast. Most horses will clear the water easily if given the chance to measure their stride.

◀ **Home-made jump**
The pole and oil-drum jump is a classic for practise at home. The only drawback is that it is not easy to vary the height. But for the early stages of jumping it is ideal.

Showing a horse

Most local shows run a variety of classes suitable for a novice rider's show-ring debut, and it is probably wisest initially to choose a show class rather than a jumping class. A utility horse class, for instance, will give the rider ring experience and the opportunity to jump one or two fences without the pressure of jumping an entire round.

When the rider is eventually proficient enough to compete in minor show-jumping competitions it is best to avoid the very small shows and aim at those which are using approved standard jumps. Flimsy fences and badly-built courses will positively hinder a horse, and a well-built solid course is far more inviting and easier to jump.

Nervousness at your entry into competitive riding and the intimidating effect of seeing fences that you have not constructed yourself, may cause you to alter your style of riding at first. Try not to communicate this to your horse. Give him plenty of time to see his fences and do not be unusually forceful in the approach to the jumps. Walk the course beforehand, and remind yourself that you have jumped fences just as big at home.

SHOW CLASSES

There is hardly a breed of horse which would not be eligible for a class in the show ring. Many of the classes have been formed to encourage breed improvement. This is particularly true of *Arabs* and the *mountain and moorland ponies*. But there are other classes, held at shows of various importance, for animals whose function is more important than their breed. At smaller shows, for example, *utility and family horses, riding club horses* and *children's ponies* all have a chance to complete. The judges will be looking for good conformation, straightforward action and a pleasant, responsive ride. *Ridden hunters* and *working hunters* are very popular and well-subscribed classes. Ridden hunters are classified by weight with additional classes for novices and ladies (to be ridden side-saddle). Working hunters are required to jump a course of fences before being judged for conformation and ride. *Show ponies* are judges in three categories: up to 12.1hh, up to 14.2hh and up to 14.2hh. They are judged at all paces and on the way they are turned out and handled by their riders.

Preparing for your first show

Having decided which showing class to enter, the rider must work out a plan for the individual show. The golden rule is never to attempt anything too ambitious. If your mount is reluctant to rein-back, for instance, don't be tempted to include this.

Basically the judge wants to see that your horse goes willingly forward in all paces, responding to the aids in upwards and downwards transitions, and, depending on the class, has the ability to jump small fences.

A simple show could begin with a brisk walk from the line-up, followed by a figure of eight in trot, with the rider remembering to ride on the correct diagonal, and change it at the centre of the figure. This could be followed by a smooth transition to a large canter circle with a change of rein, through trot, across the diagonal. Correct canter leads are vital, so full use should be made of corners for transitions. If the ring has any slope at all, the gallop or extension should take place along the longest *uphill* side, and by the time the corner is reached the horse should have come back kindly to canter. *Never* gallop downhill or near the other horses.

If there is a jump it can be slotted in when canter is re-established after the gallop. At the end of a display the horse should be halted near to the judge, a few steps of rein-back shown, and the rider should then bow, smile at the judge, pat the horse and return to the line.

In a class of this sort the horse can be shown either in a double bridle or a snaffle. A double bridle obviously looks more showy, but should be used only by an experienced rider, particularly if jumping is involved.

The ring experience gained in showing classes will stand the novice rider in good stead for jumping classes and, at the same time, a great deal of fun can be had!

75

Riding a dressage test

Another competition well within the capabilities of most improving riders is the preliminary dressage test, which will involve only school movements with which most riders are familiar, having practised them frequently.

Copies of the tests used are available at very small cost from your national equestrian society, but the rider should not make the mistake of practising the complete test at home because the horse has an excellent memory and will quickly learn the sequence of movements. Valuable marks will be lost if the horse anticipates the aids and begins a movement prematurely.

The rider should be clear on the positions of the markers and, if possible, practise the movements individually, or in a different order, in a manège the size of a dressage arena, which is 40 metres by 20 metres.

One of the useful aspects of dressage tests is that the judges mark and comment on each individual movement, and the rider should study these written comments and learn from them.

Dressage tests can be fun and, as with showing classes, give both horse and rider valuable ring experience.

The dressage test
The exercises which form the basis of all dressage competitions have been developed to improve the suppleness and obedience of the horse. Since they are also used for the training of riders, there is no reason why anyone should be afraid of dressage. The stylised ring shown here, indicates that the dressage manége is almost identical to the school.

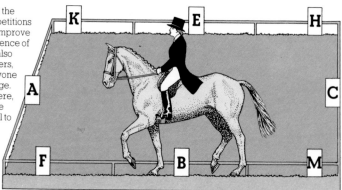

In this section we introduce movements and competitive work that many riders may never aspire to. On the other hand, they are the kind of activities which will be of benefit to any rider. Nothing included here is beyond the rider of average ability, but it is advisable to be proficient in all the preceding stages before moving on to this one.

MORE COMPLEX MOVEMENTS

As work on the basic paces and school movements continues, other slightly more complex movements should be introduced in order to improve co-ordination and understanding of the aids.

Simple change, in which the horse is asked to change the leg with which it leads in canter, is an excellent exercise in making smooth transitions through the gaits, or paces. Being able to rein back is of considerable practical value. When riding in the countryside, there are many occasions on which it will be much more convenient to make the horse step back rather than turn.

Turn on the forehand is of great value to the rider, but of rather less to the horse. It improves the rider's co-ordination and supplies an introduction to lateral work, besides being useful for opening gates when out hacking. It does tend, however, to bring the horse onto the forehand and should be practised for short periods only. Immediately after any movements of this nature, including rein-back, the horse should be sent actively forward.

Simple change

Simple change, whereby the canter lead is changed through trot and walk across the diagonal, necessitates precise and immediate aids, because the horse, as it crosses the diagonal, must be brought from canter to trot, then walk, back into trot, and finally into canter again on the other rein. The natural tendency of the horse is to adopt the canter lead it was on moments before and this it will do if the rider does not change the bend and apply definite aids. Accurate use of the markers is very important in this, and all, movements.

The transition
In this illustration, the horse has been brought from the canter to the trot and is just coming down into the walk.

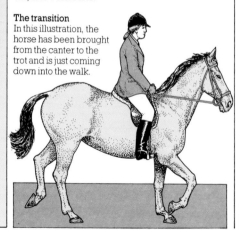

Rein back

Rein-back is a two-time movement in which the horse steps backwards with its legs moving in diagonal pairs. Before it is attempted the rider must ensure that the horse is standing attentively with a relaxed jaw and a fairly low head-carriage. The rider should apply both legs to send the horse forward, but instead of easing the hands to allow the forward movement they remain closed and, as a result, the horse steps back. The leg pressure should be even so that the horse steps backwards without swinging its hindquarters out to one side.

Turn on the forehand

To ask for a turn on the forehand to the right, the rider should firstly establish the horse in an attentive square halt with a relaxed jaw. The contact must be maintained by both hands, with the horse looking slightly to the right. The rider's right leg should be applied behind the girth in order to move the hindquarters to the left, and the left leg stays by the girth for support and to prevent the horse from moving backwards, which is a very bad fault. The right hindleg crosses in front of the left hindleg and the horse pivots on the off-fore.

Correct action
The rider's hands are kept low as the horse, with head down and drawn in, steps back.

Turn to the left
In this picture, the rider is using the left leg to send the quarters to the right. The left hind leg is crossing the right.

79

Walking & riding a course

Walking the course is an important prelude to competitive jumping, and it is a good idea for the inexperienced competitor to accompany an experienced rider.

Distances between combination fences must be paced in order to establish the number of strides allowed for, and attention must be given to the approaches of all fences. It may be necessary for the rider to bring the horse back into trot on tight turns in order not to overshoot.

All fences are numbered, with a red flag on the right-hand side, and a white flag on the left. Fences likely to cause difficulties are combinations and those which are jumped away from the collecting ring, therefore the rider must anticipate difficulties and be sure to ride an especially good approach into a combination, and to ride with a little more determination away from the collecting ring.

Before jumping the course, horse and rider will need to warm up over a practice fence in order to limber-up and put the horse into the right frame of mind for jumping. In most cases, popping over the practice fence half-a-dozen times is sufficient. If the rider does too much, or has the practice fence higher than those in the ring, the horse may have nothing left to offer once the round has actually begun.

Another situation to be avoided is standing around in the collecting ring chatting! The horse must be kept alert and moving, otherwise the warm-up will have been for nothing.

Once in the ring, the rider should trot and canter around the jumps until the starting bell goes, and then circle widely to the first fence in order to secure a good approach. The first fence, despite being inviting and lower than the others, is, nevertheless, the most difficult on the course, so firm, determined riding is vital. The rider must remember throughout the round to use the space given and ride into the corners, and also to look at the next fence at all times. A clear round first time out is unlikely, but fun is guaranteed!

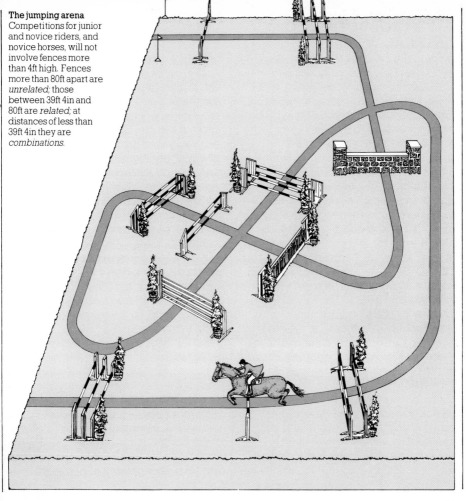

The jumping arena
Competitions for junior and novice riders, and novice horses, will not involve fences more than 4ft high. Fences more than 80ft apart are *unrelated;* those between 39ft 4in and 80ft are *related;* at distances of less than 39ft 4in they are *combinations.*

AN INTRODUCTION TO LATERAL WORK

Movements such as *shoulder-in* and *half-pass* come under the heading of lateral work and may be introduced when the rider has reached a fairly high standard, and advanced to riding horses schooled to a higher level.

In lateral work the horse moves on two tracks with the forehand always in advance of the quarters, is bent from the poll to the tail, and looks in the direction in which it is going.

The lateral movements supple all parts of the horse and improve its balance and obedience to the rider's aids. They should, however, be practised for short periods only, and introduced when horse and rider have warmed-up and progressed through a series of exercises such as circles and quick-succession transitions, so that the horse is alert, on the bit, and ready for the work. After lateral work the horse should be sent energetically straight forward.

Turn on the forehand (see page 79) will have been used as the rider's first introduction to lateral work, and this can be followed by *leg-yielding* to give the rider the feel of the horse moving forwards and sideways at the same time.

Leg yielding

Before the rider asks for leg-yielding, the horse should be walking actively forward with impulsion, and the rider should come onto the threequarter line of the manège, i.e., well to the inside of the track. The horse must be straight and when it reaches the half-marker (B or E) the rider should apply the inside leg behind the girth, asking the horse to step forwards and sideways to the outside track. The outside leg should be used on the girth to maintain the forward movement; and the exercise can later be carried out in sitting trot.

Leg-yielding, like all other exercises, must be performed on both reins. It is not true lateral work, but an introduction, and therefore the horse is required to look forwards with no bend in the head or neck. Leg-yielding can also be practised whilst out hacking, with the rider asking the horse to step forwards and sideways along a wide track, remembering that the horse must be straight to begin with, and to ask only for a few steps at a time.

It is, of course, logical to move on to such manoeuvres as the half-pass and shoulder-in: the leg-yielding exercise is, after all, a preparation for them. But be prepared to give your horse plenty of practise at the simpler movement first.

Leg yielding
Here, the rider is using the inside leg behind the girth to send the horse to the left, but the other leg is on the girth to maintain forward movement.

SHOULDER-IN/HALF PASS

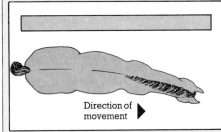

Direction of movement ▶

Shoulder-in
In this movement, the horse moves with its hind feet and fore feet on separate tracks. The horse's body is bent as it moves at an angle of about 35° to the direction of movement.

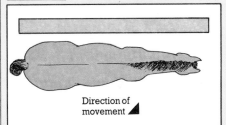

Direction of movement ◢

Half pass
This movement requires the horse to travel obliquely with only the slightest flexion of the body towards the direction of travel. The horse crosses one leg in front of the other, but this is still a forward, rather than a sideways, movement.

Cross country riding

Cross-country riding can be great fun and local hunter trials offer the ideal event for the improving rider's inauguration to this thrilling sport.

Unlike show jumping, cross-country fences are solid and will not fall if hit, but to compensate for this they are inviting to the horse and generally lower than show jumps. Also, unlike show jumping, the pace used on a cross-country course is the gallop rather than the canter.

Gallop is a pace of four-time and the rider asks for gallop by extending the horse from canter. Unless the horse is resisting going forward, the rider should adopt a forward position to allow complete freedom to the horse's back and loins. The rider's weight should be taken on the knee, with the ankle acting as a shock absorber and the stirrup leather vertical.

Most horses galloping cross-country are keener than usual, and the rider must work progressively through trot and canter, with the horse well between hand and leg, before advancing to gallop. The rider should not be looking for a flat-out gallop, but for a steady, controlled, rhythmical pace, both uphill and down.

THE CROSS-COUNTRY EVENT

Prepare yourself

Prepare your horse

Preparation
Arrive early at the location of the event, let your horse settle down and give him a drink if there is an hour or more before the competition. Walk the course and familiarise yourself with the obstacles. Tack up your horse in plenty of time, putting on bandages or jumping boots if they are necessary. Warm up thoroughly, and keep your mount on the move right up to the 'off'.

Galloping position
Sit forward and take your weight on the knee. Keep your hands low and your legs and ankles flexed.

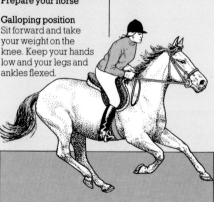

The cross-country course

The fences are designed to be more 'natural' than show jumps, but they are usually lower. Banks, ditches, treetrunks, gates, stiles and walls are frequently encountered.

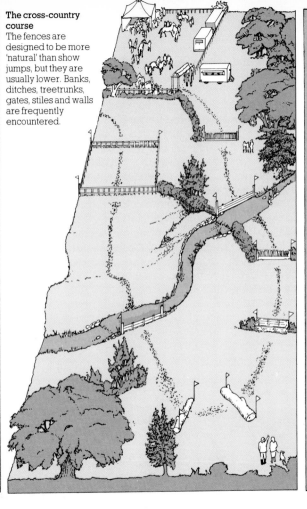

TYPICAL FENCES

The fences shown below represent a fairly simple course. In a novice competition there may be 20 such fences to jump, and at a speed of 33 kph (20 mph).

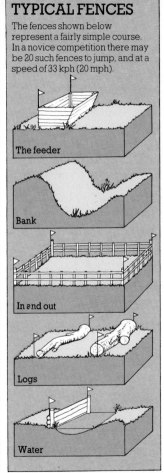

The feeder

Bank

In and out

Logs

Water

85

Improving the horse

As the rider progresses, achieving true independence of hands and seat, and that other most important quality, feel, another aspect of horsemanship will open its doors; the ability to improve the horse rather than just to ride it.

A good rider can improve virtually any horse, either out hacking or working in a manège. In the latter case, for instance, the rider can lighten the horse's forehand by encouraging it to work with its hocks well engaged and in a round outline, by means of progressive suppling exercises and sympathetic co-ordination of the aids. One of the many possible exercises consists of quick-succession transitions whereby the rider takes the horse repeatedly from *trot to canter,* from *canter to trot,* completing about six strides of each established pace before changing. This

sharpens the horse's responses and brings it off the forehand and on to the bit.

While out hacking the rider can work the horse forward actively at all paces, make good use of hills for improving balance, and work the horse on straight lines in even, rhythmical paces.

Some horses, of course, will respond more easily than others, and the rider may have to work very hard to gain just a little improvement. The rewards in riding are many and varied and achieving a desired movement, or simply feeling the incredible difference as a horse comes on to the bit, are magic moments indeed, as exciting to the improving rider as achieving their first clear round or cantering victoriously round the show ring clutching their first rosette.

Transitions
These diagrams show how the horse changes its action from walk to trot, from trot to canter and from canter back to trot.

GLOSSARY/INDEX

Many newcomers to riding are confused by the language of 'horsy' people. Like most other areas of specialised interest, the world of equitation uses terms and expressions which may seem odd or unnecessary to the uninitiated. Nevertheless, a familiarity with the basic technical terms is helpful in talking about, and dealing with, horses. You will find that it is also unavoidable. The following pages list some, but by no means all, of the words that you will come across.

Glossary of terms

AIDS
The signals by which the rider makes known his wishes to the horse. Natural aids include the hands, legs, body and voice. Artificial aids are spurs, whips and martingales.

ANTHELMINTICS
Chemically composed worming agents, administered either in the feed or by stomach tube.

BACKING
The act of putting a rider on a young horse for the first time.

BED DOWN
Laying a bed in a stable for a horse.

BITLESS BRIDLE (Hackamore)
A bridle which controls the horse by pressure on the nose.

BLOOM
The shine on a horse's coat.

BOG SPAVIN
A soft swelling to the front of the inner side of the hock.

BONE SPAVIN
A bony enlargement on the lower aspect of the inside of the hock.

BOOT HOOK
Metal hooks which pass through the webbing straps on the inside of leather top boots in order to assist the wearer with pulling them on.

BOOT JACK
A piece of shaped wood, generally with a rubber grip, used for pulling leather top boots off.

BREAKING IN
The process of training the young horse to accept the rider or go in harness.

BROKEN KNEES
Injury to the horse's knees as a result of stumbling or falling.

BROOD MARE
A mare used for breeding.

BRUSHING
The striking of one leg by the opposite leg.

CANNON BONE
The straight bone which runs down from the knee or hock to the fetlock. Often termed the Shannon Bone on the hindleg.

CAPPED ELBOW
A large, painless soft swelling on the elbow caused by bruising.

CAPPED HOCK
A large, painless soft swelling on the point of the hock caused by bruising.

CAST
When a horse is unable to get up in its box, probably due to lying down too near to the wall.

CLENCH
The projecting end of the nail used to secure a shoe.

COLT
A young male horse of three years or under.

CONTACT
The feeling between the rider's hands and the horse's mouth via the reins.

CREST
The ridge along the top of the horse's neck, more pronounced in stallions, or geldings which were castrated later than usual.

CUP
The metal holder attached to the jump stand in which the pole lies.

DOUBLE BRIDLE
A bridle equipped with two bits: a *curb* and a *snaffle*. Each bit has its own cheek pieces and reins. Much used for showing, dressage and show jumping, double bridles encourage the horse to keep its head up and nose in.

DROPPED NOSEBAND
A noseband whose back strap passes below the mouthpiece of the bit. Used in conjunction with the snaffle, it prevents the horse getting its tongue over the bit or opening its mouth to evade the contact.

EVASION
The act of trying to avoid the rider's instructions through the aids – not merely resisting.

FILLY
A young female horse of three years or under.

FORGING
The act of the hind shoe striking the fore shoe, usually in trot.

FROG
The V-shaped anti-slipping and anti-concussion formation in the sole of the horse's foot.

FULLERED
A term used to describe a shoe whose ground surface is provided with a groove.

GELDING
A castrated male horse.

GESTATION
The period of time between conception and birth. In a horse this period is around 340 days or 11 months.

GIRTH
The strap which passes underneath the horse in order to keep the saddle in place.

GOOSE RUMP
A description of a horse whose quarters slope acutely from the highest point to the root of the tail.

HACKAMORE
A bitless bridle whereby the horse is controlled by pressure on the nose.

Glossary of terms

HEADCOLLAR
Headgear (not a bridle) used to restrain the horse. Generally made of leather or nylon.

HOGGING
The complete removal of the mane with clippers.

INTERNATIONAL RIDERS' CLUB
A club formed in the mid 1970's to which almost all the leading international show jumpers belong.

KNEE-CAPS
Felt pads bound and strapped on with leather, used as protection for the knee during travelling or exercise.

LEY
A mixture of hay and grasses specifically sown for cutting or grazing.

LOG
Wooden block fastened to the end of a rope passing through a ring, in order to secure a horse in a stall.

LUNGEING
The act of sending a horse or pony (with or without a rider) around the trainer in a circle.

MARE
A female horse aged 4 years or more.

MARTINGALE
A device which is used to prevent the horse throwing its head in the air – thus evading the bit. It consists of a strap which connects the girth to the noseband (standing martingale), or from the girth to a ring on each rein (running martingale).

MUCKING OUT
The daily task of removing droppings and soiled straw from the stable.

MULLEN MOUTHPIECE
Unjointed snaffle mouthpiece, slightly curved. Also known as half-moon.

NAPPING
Resistance offered by the horse, such as refusing to leave other horses or enter the show-ring.

NAVICULAR
A serious disease process of the navicular bone, usually confined to the forefeet.

NUMNAH
A pad, usually of sheepskin, which is placed under the saddle to prevent rubbing.

OVER-REACH
A wound caused by the toe of the hind shoe striking the heel of the front foot. A common jumping injury.

Glossary of terms

PULLING
The act of shortening the mane and tidying the top of the tail by pulling out hair.

PULSE
The normal pulse rate for horses is around 36 – 42 beats per minute.

QUARTERING
Early morning grooming consisting of picking out the feet, sponging the eyes, nostrils and dock, throwing up the back and front parts of the rug and brushing the exposed coat, and the removal of stable stains. The whole process is completed without undoing the rug, roller or surcingle.

QUIDDING
The act of the horse dropping particles and lumps of food from its mouth, usually caused by problems with the teeth.

REIN BACK
A two-time movement in which the horse steps backwards, the legs moving in diagonal pairs.

RUGGING-UP
Putting rugs on a horse.

SIDE BONE
Bony enlargements in the heel region.

SPLINTS
Bony enlargements involving the splint and cannon bones.

STALING
The term used for a horse urinating.

STALLION
An entire male horse aged 4 years or more.

STUDS
Metal studs screwed into the shoes to prevent the horse slipping. Also the name given to an establishment where horses are bred.

SWEET ITCH
A troublesome disease caused by sensitisation to biting flies or midges.

TEMPERATURE
The normal temperature for the horse is 100.5°F or 38°C.

WOLF TEETH
Rudimentary teeth situated in front of the upper and lower molars which are often removed because they interfere with the bit, causing the horse pain.

Index

Index

Index

INDEX OF RIDING INSTRUCTION

Acknowledgments

The 'How To' Book of Riding and
Horse Care was created by
Simon Jennings and Company Limited.
We are grateful to the following
individuals and organisations
for their assistance in the
making of this book:

Nigel Chamberlain: *all line and tone illustrations*
John Couzins: *cover and title page photographs*
The Dover Archive: *engravings and embellishments*
Ann Hall: *compilation of index*
Peter Mackertich: *photograph page 21*
Marta Jennings: *additional artwork*
George Parker & Sons (Saddlers) Ltd., London: *for the loan of
riding tack and equipment*
Michael Woods: *all colour illustrations*
Zefa Picture Library: *all colour photographs*

Thanks to Marie Stokes, Carol Green and Caroline Newman
of the Walton Heath Livery Stables, Surrey, for the
provision of stable facilities and riding demonstration.

Typesetting by Text Filmsetters Ltd., Orpington, Kent
Headline setting by Diagraphic Typesetting Ltd., London
Additional display setting by Facet Photosetting, London

Special thanks to Norman Ruffell and
the staff of Swaingrove Ltd., Bury St. Edmunds,
Suffolk, for the lithographic reproduction.